# JOHN STEINBREDER

# 18
# WAYS TO PLAY A
# BETTER 18 HOLES

## Tips and Techniques from America's Best Club Professionals

TAYLOR TRADE PUBLISHING

*Lanham • Boulder • New York • Toronto • Plymouth, UK*

Published by Taylor Trade Publishing
An imprint of Rowman & Littlefield
4501 Forbes Boulevard, Suite 200, Lanham, Maryland 20706
www.rowman.com

10 Thornbury Road, Plymouth PL6 7PP, United Kingdom

Distributed by National Book Network

British Library Cataloguing in Publication Information Available

**Library of Congress Cataloging-in-Publication Data**
Steinbreder, John.
   18 ways to play a better 18 holes : tips and techniques from America's best club professionals / John Steinbreder.
      pages cm
   Includes index.
   ISBN 978-1-58979-774-1 (pbk.) — ISBN 978-1-58979-775-8 (electronic) 1. Golf—Training.
I. Title. II. Title: Eighteen ways to play a better eighteen holes.
   GV979.T68S79 2014
   796.352'3—dc23
                                                                        2013030862

∞™ The paper used in this publication meets the minimum requirements of American National Standard for Information Sciences—Permanence of Paper for Printed Library Materials, ANSI/NISO Z39.48-1992.

Printed in the United States of America

# 18
# WAYS TO PLAY A BETTER 18 HOLES

# Contents

# CONTENTS

# Introduction

No one knows or understands the game of golf quite as well as a PGA of America club professional. In most cases, he or she is introduced to the game as a youngster, usually by caddying or teeing it up with relatives who like to play. Once he determines he wants to make a living in golf, he goes on to study the sport in college, learning its managerial and instructional nuances at any of the two dozen or so prestigious universities in the United States that offer PGM (for PGA Professional Golf Management) programs. And he hones those skills he acquires in class in the real golf world when his schooling is done, toiling at clubs and resorts and learning about everything from organizing tournaments and selling merchandise to running clinics and interacting with members. Even when he completes his formal education, his studying is not done, and he goes through a wide range of courses and clinics offered by the PGA as he progresses as a club pro in an effort to further even more his knowledge of the game as he expands his skill sets.

Throughout this time, the club professional also works hard to become a first-rate player, competing in regional and national tournaments and spending hours trying to improve his own game when he is not helping others do the same with theirs. He thinks constantly about the ways he can make golf more enjoyable and entertaining for players, and he comes to devote his entire professional life to promoting and advancing the sport he knows and loves.

The PGA professional works with the very best players as well as with rank beginners. He scrutinizes swing videos and reads books and magazine articles that break down different ideas and theories in order to broaden his intellectual horizons. He spends hours on practice ranges, watching golfers hit balls and taking note of the ways each ball reacts when it flies off the clubface. He talks incessantly with fellow professionals about the things they've all learned about golf instruction over the years—and the things they want to know and discover. He tries to sort out the intricate mental aspects of the sport and relate the different ways golfers can improve in that area, too. In essence, he and his colleagues are professors of the highest order, with golfing PhDs and not only the remarkable ability to dissect and discern golf swings and provide psychological counsel but also the skill to impart that knowledge to their students in clear and concise ways.

There is nothing quite like a PGA club professional. And that is why I have turned to 18 of the best ones in the United States to relate 18 ways to play a better 18 holes. It's as if I have gone to the faculties of Stanford, Yale, and Princeton and selected the finest teachers from those institutions, a sort of instructional dream team. It's like my taking readers to the best and most exclusive clubs and giving them insight and information available heretofore only to members who pay thousands of dollars a year to belong to those ultraprivate retreats—but for the mere price of a hardcover book or a digital download.

One of the members of that team is Bob Ford of the Oakmont Country Club and the Seminole Golf Club, perhaps the most revered and respected club professional in the game, for both his teaching and playing prowess. And in this book, he publicly shares his secrets on bunker play for the first time. His protégé Jack Druga, the head professional at Shinnecock Hills Golf Club, is here, too, outlining the all-important but all too poorly understood imperatives of effective practice. The Deepdale Golf Club's Darrell Kestner is regarded as not only one of the great golf instructors in the United States but also one of the best club professional players in the over-50 realm. And here he is, offering his thoughts on how to better compete, whether you are an elite amateur looking to win a national stroke play tournament or a weekend hacker simply trying to makes a few bucks off your golfing buddies when they play their Saturday morning Nassaus. Brendan Walsh of The Country Club in Brookline, Massachusetts, is a contributor as well, discussing in his chapter the virtues of club fitting and the best ways to have that done properly. Suzy Whaley of TPC River Highlands in Cromwell, Connecticut, is here, too, offering pointers on how to take effective lessons. Then there is Eden Foster, of the Maidstone Club on Long Island, detailing the best ways to hit pure irons and hybrids.

The information is this book is as wide ranging as it is astute. Consider, for example, Bob Rittberger of the Garden City Golf Club outside New York City, who imparts his knowledge on the critical matter of course management. Bill Stines of Scioto Country Club in Columbus, Ohio, the place where Jack Nicklaus learned to play the game, has essential advice on fitness and conditioning, while Paul Marchand, the longtime coach of Fred Couples and Colin Montgomerie, brings readers right onto the professional tours with his revelations on how the pros operate so successfully and what we, as mere golfing mortals, can learn from them.

To be sure, this is a unique publishing approach. I am not relying on the teachings and philosophies of an individual professional or espousing one teaching theory. Nor am I concentrating on a single aspect of the game. Rather, I am covering a vast area of golf instruction, ranging from swing mechanics to mental discipline, and doing so with an all-star roster of teaching pros.

Consider what we are offering in chapter 7, with Scott Nye, head professional at the historic Merion Golf Club, site of the 2013 US Open. He has developed an approach he calls "finding five," in which he works with his members in very unconventional sessions before and after their rounds to find ways throughout the golf season to reduce their scores by five strokes. It's about making better swings, of course, but also course management and creating realistic expectations, setting goals, and analyzing results to see what could be done differently and better next time around. "The idea is to see a progression, and to work on lowering their scores each time they are out on the golf course as they also increase the amount of fun they are having there," Nye says. "It's not about pounding balls on the range and trying to hit the perfect shot. The game is about getting the golf ball in the hole, and 'finding five' is about helping my students do that better. It's about making a plan for a round beforehand and then assessing afterwards how they followed that, why they hit certain shots, and what the results were."

My feeling is that this volume will be consumed in a couple of ways. Some readers will go through it from start to finish, while others are likely to choose chapters on much more of an "a la carte" basis, turning to those subjects that interest them the most—and that cover the areas in which they need the most assistance. Whatever their approach, I feel sure they will derive real help and knowledge the first time they go through this publication, and believe they will find it just as useful as a reference they can turn to time and time again.

The PGA club professionals who contributed to this book have provided some extraordinarily deep and useful material. To acquire that, I interviewed each one personally and then put their ideas, concepts, theories, and insights into words. Once that was completed, I shared drafts of their chapters with them and then incorporated any additions, deletions, or amplifications they might have had into a finished product.

The result of those efforts is this book, and the PGA professionals who worked on these chapters have provided Ivy League–quality educations and ultraprivate club access. They have offered up 18 good and effective ways to play a better 18 holes.

It is time to take advantage of all that.

# CHAPTER ONE

# Driving

## Scott Davenport, Quail Hollow Club

Ben Hogan once said that the driving was the most critical shot in golf, and he had a pretty good point, especially when he added that you really couldn't play the game if you could not get off the tee with any proficiency. We also know that even if we are not scoring well, there is still something quite satisfying about hitting one good tee shot after another. It can compensate for a lot of other golfing ills.

Scott Davenport, Quail Hollow Club

In addition, there may not be a club in the bag that players like to hit so much, whether on the golf course or off the practice tee. What that means, of course, is that hitting a drive is generally as popular as it is important.

Of course, we can make a fairly strong case for putting being the most critical shot in golf, and understandably so. Putts generally account for about 40 percent of the shots made in an average round, and we all know that putting is what separates the great touring professionals from the merely good, to say nothing of what it means to competitions at lower levels. Quite simply, you win if you can putt. But even if some might insist that putting is number one, then driving has to be considered a very close second. And even if it is number two, it remains a critically vital part of a golfer's repertoire.

Why? Golf these days is in many ways a distance game, and producing distance off the tee is essential. It's that way at the pro and elite amateur level, to be sure, though strong ball striking and deft short-game play can overcome lapses in length. And it is an even bigger deal with club and recreational golf. Anybody who can hit the ball 20, or 30, or even 40 yards past his opponents in those types of settings is generally the one who has the best chances to win.

Distance in golf is all about clubhead speed, and like speed in any other sport, it can be a tremendous advantage. It is also the result of solid contact, and I have found over the years that you cannot produce distance if you are stiff and tight. No one spoke to that point as well as Jackie Burke, who once said that you should swing your drive as if you were trying to hit the ball into the Atlantic Ocean. His point is that he wanted players to swing as freely and easily as possible, with little regard for where the ball is going. The best drivers, in his mind, felt that way, and being carefree in that way allowed them to make the best possible swings—and generate the highest clubhead speeds. And he rightly thought that a golfer must let go of some control to produce distance.

Another critical element of distance is producing a ball flight that is curving from right to left, for a right-handed player. Any shot bending to the right will go shorter than one going left and will encourage a swing traveling across the ball, which does not allow a player to hit the golf ball square. To hit a drive curving left, one that produces a draw, a golfer has to swing from the inside, which creates a shallow angle of approach into the ball. That also means that the right elbow and right wrist are forced to stay bent until it is time to hit the ball.

In my view, the ideal launch condition for optimal driving distance is a tee shot hit high into the air with minimal backspin. And that comes from striking the ball from the inside with the face slightly closed. Making a full turn and swing will also help with the clubhead speed element. To do that properly, the back should be turned to the target in the backswing, with the shoulders and chest turning well left of the target as the swing moves forward. The sequence of the turn in the forward swing starts with the lower body, but the feeling is that everything turns together. The shoulders will turn twice as much as the hips going back, so there is no need to hold back going through. The combination of the full turn with the arms feeling like spaghetti should allow you to produce maximum speed.

Golfers can also help bolster their clubhead speeds when they hit their drivers and other clubs in their bags by working on their strength and flexibility in the gym. A good PGA club professional will be able to help you devise a program to do both of those or direct you to a place where you can do that, and added yards on your drivers should follow.

I mentioned earlier that if distance is properly and correctly produced, then direction is easily controlled. When the best golfers hit their drives, they are using all their muscles, but none at near half their capacity. The free swing and turn in the backswing facilitates the unwinding of the body in the forward swing, and centrifugal force releases the club.

All of this is made much easier by a stronger grip, one where both hands are rotated to the right of the clubface. The stronger grip allows for a full hinging of the wrists in the backswing and a delayed unhinging in the downswing. Rarely will you see a long driver who does not have a strong grip, one where the *V*s formed by the thumb and forefinger of each hand point toward the right shoulder.

Another huge upside to the stronger grip is that the clubface stays squarer throughout the swing with one. This means that the player can be less concerned about direction. He is also able to help himself in that regard simply by relaxing and appreciating that he has anywhere from 25 to 40 yards to play with in terms of direction when he looks down a fairway. That's the size of most golf course fairways. And that should give him plenty of room in which to operate. That should give him the Jackie Burke–like sense of the ocean.

Scott Davenport is the head professional at the Quail Hollow Club in Charlotte, North Carolina. *Golf Digest* recently ranked him among the top ten instructors in the state.

# CHAPTER TWO

# Bunker Play

## Bob Ford, Oakmont Country Club/ Seminole Golf Club

In many ways, a bunker shot may be the easiest shot in golf because it is the only one you make where you do not actually have to hit the ball. You just have to hit the sand behind it and go under the ball, using a full swing. It's that simple, yet we find that many players are still quite intimidated by those shots. They try so hard to help their golf balls out of the sand and onto the green, and as a

Bob Ford, Oakmont Country Club
and Seminole Golf Club

result, they have a tendency to "scoop" them. But when they do that, they hit too far behind their golf balls, which causes players either to hit them fat or to skull them.

It doesn't have to be that way, though. Bunker shots really aren't that difficult.

I've found over the years that the vast majority of golfers just want to get out and on from greenside bunkers. And with that goal in mind, they need only apply what I call "bunker play 101." It's an approach I developed from more than 30 years as a head professional and from the opportunities I have had to observe and work with some real masters of bunker play—like Lew Worsham, the winner of the 1947 US Open and the longtime Oakmont professional I succeeded, and Jerry Pitman, my predecessor at Seminole who held the head professional position at that club for nearly 30 years after having played the PGA Tour for more than a decade. They were great bunker players, and they were very good at teaching people how to be proficient bunker players themselves, which makes sense when you consider those clubs, each of which have some 200 bunkers. You had to know how to play bunker shots if you worked at those places, and you had to know how to teach your members how to do so as well. Over the years, I also spent a lot of time listening to the Harmon brothers—Dick, Butch, and Craig—and absorbing their theories on bunker play as well as the ones developed by their father, Claude, the winner of the 1948 Masters who also served as the head professional at Seminole and Winged Foot, which has a pair of courses that also put a premium on good bunker play. All of that amounted to an extraordinary education on how to get out of the sand, and it helped me develop what I call BP 101.

You start by positioning the ball under the logo of your shirt, assuming you are a right-handed player. Open the clubface slightly to increase loft, and then open your feet slightly to compensate for the open clubface. Then, use your normal full swing—and your normal finish—to blast the ball out of the bunker and onto the green, again being sure to hit behind the ball and then go under it. It really is that simple.

I have a favorite drill to help players improve their bunker play, and it entails drawing a line in the sand, and then putting a golf ball an inch or two in front of the line. That is where your entry point should be. Golfers have a tendency to bottom out too early in the sand in an effort to get the ball onto the green, and this drill helps them see the more optimal place to make contact.

As I mentioned previously, the majority of golfers are happy just to get their golf balls out of the sand and onto the green. That's a good approach from a psychological standpoint that keeps expectations somewhat low and helps to make them less fearful of those shots. And it makes sense when you consider they likely lack the physical skills to do much more than that. But there are those better players who are also looking to get their golf balls close to the holes, who are trying to be more precise. And to do those things effectively and consistently, they need to make other considerations.

One is the type and condition of the sand, and it is important to take note of those factors when you step into a bunker and walk to your golf ball. That will help you determine how and where you hit a particular bunker shot. If the sand is thicker, wetter, or fluffier, you will have to take a fuller swing because the ball will likely not go as far. You will probably want to fly your shot closer to the pin, as the ball will be less likely to run and roll. And you will want to be especially careful not to take too much sand. If, however, the sand is sparser, you will want to take a somewhat abbreviated swing, and you should count on the ball running a bit more, which means you don't want to land it so close to the hole.

No matter what your ability, however, regardless of whether you are part of the broader 90 percent or the elite 10, you can help the way you play your shots out of the bunkers by practicing them with different types of swings and in different kinds of sand with various levels of thickness and consistency. The more you do that, the more you get comfortable with your bunker shots and the ways your golf balls react when you hit them from those hazards, the better your play on the golf course will be. And the lower your scores.

Not surprisingly, the approach to bunker play differs somewhat as you find yourself farther from the green. For most golfers, I suggest they stick with the BP 101 theory, even as they find themselves with shots 30, 40, and 50 yards in length, opening up the clubface a bit and taking the same backswing and finishing with the same follow-through, only using a club that has less loft. And keep decreasing loft as you get farther away from the hole. As for fairway bunkers, I suggest playing shots out of them just as you would off the fairway itself, swinging as if you were taking a divot, as opposed to lifting the ball out of the sand. Generally speaking, it makes sense to go up a club when you are hitting from a fairway bunker to compensate for the distance you will likely lose from playing out of the sand.

I have heard lots of stories over the years about great bunker play, and my favorite is one about Moe Norman, the talented and eccentric Canadian golf professional often considered one of the best ball strikers in the history of the game. He was playing the final hole of the Canadian

PGA Championship one year with another great player from that country, George Knudson. Moe was holding a two-shot lead, and as he walked up the 18th green, he heard Knudson rave about a young South African player he had recently seen play, saying he was perhaps the best bunker player in the world. Both Norman and Knudson were on the green in regulation, and Norman was away. But instead of putting to the hole, he hit his ball backward into a greenside bunker. Then, he walked into the bunker, played his shot to tap-in range, drained his putt to win the championship, and walked over to Knudson to say: "I'm the best bunker player in the world, and don't you forget it!"

People ask me all the time what wedge works best for bunker shots around the green, and that's a good question because we have so many options these days, from 52 degrees to 64 degrees and everything in between. Bounce is also a consideration, and there are as many variations of that as well. To determine what is best for you, I recommend you talk with the professional at your club or course. But don't let yourself get too confused by all the choices. For 90 percent of golfers and BP 101, the standard 56-degree sand wedge with anywhere from 12 to 16 degrees of bounce is all they need.

Bob Ford is the head golf professional at the Oakmont Country Club outside Pittsburgh, Pennsylvania, and the Seminole Golf Club in Juno Beach, Florida. He is regarded as not only a fine teacher but also a first-rate merchandiser and an excellent player who has qualified for ten PGA Championships and three US Opens. Ford has won ten PGA Tri-State section Player of the Year awards and has been named national PGA Club Professional of the Year as well as national PGA Club Professional Player of the Year.

# CHAPTER THREE

# Effective Practice

## Jack Druga, Shinnecock Hills Golf Club

We all know practice is important if we want to get better at golf. But we all have such restrictions on our time today, working as hard as we do and with so many family commitments. And even when we can get away to hit balls, we do not always make the most efficient use of our time on the range or short-game areas. It is important, then, to understand the concept of effective practice.

Jack Druga is the head golf professional at the Shinnecock Hills Golf Club in Southampton, New York, site of the 2018 US Open.

To far too many golfers, practice entails little more than hitting a bucket or bag of balls from the same spot with the same club. But that is no way to improve. Here's what I suggest instead. First, pick out a target with every shot you hit. But be sure not to hit more than three balls to the same target. Second, do not hit more than ten balls with the same club. Let's face it, we all get bored when we are hitting golf balls to the same target with the same club. We all get complacent doing that. This is a way of building focus. It also makes practicing a lot more interesting.

And while we are on the subject of focus, I tell my students that if they have a preshot routine when they play the golf course, they should employ it during their practice as well. It is a good way to build consistency and solidify focus while establishing a mental routine.

I used to hear stories about Ben Hogan, who, as we all know, was famous for all the practicing he did, for finding the secrets to the golf swing in the dirt of the range. He'd put balls far enough away from him when he was working on his game that he always had to move to get them. Even if only a couple of steps. That kept him from hitting balls too quickly during his practice sessions or from the same spot. That ensured that he went through his normal preparation with each shot—and thought carefully about where and how he was hitting them.

Another excellent approach is to take different angles on a shot or to take a club with which you are not very comfortable. Too often, golfers tend to hit the shots and clubs they like the best, but that is not as helpful as it may seem. Neither is hitting balls off of perfectly flat turf or fluffed up lies. Practice shots instead off of sidehill lies. Try a few knockdown shots into the wind or a few balls out of divots.

I believe that one of the really tough things to teach in golf, one of the really hard things for golfers to learn, is what their shots are going to do out of the rough. How will the ball fly? How far will it go? So one thing I recommend is to go off to the side of the range and hit some balls out of the rough in different conditions and with different clubs. Don't you think Seve Ballesteros did that all the time? Where do you think he learned to hit all those crazy recovery shots?

Now that is what I call practicing. So is re-creating shots that give you trouble or have given you trouble in the past. Go to your PGA professional and ask him or her how to hit those. Maybe a long iron out of the rough, or a fairway metal out of a fairway bunker. Seriously, when was the last time you practiced something like that?

Players often ask me whether my recommendations for effective practice are any different for the short game and shots from, say, 50 yards in, and the answer is: not really. In fact, I like the idea of doing more or less the same thing with short wedges as with fuller swing shots, which is to aim at specific targets with three consecutive shots and then move on to another target. Never more than three wedges to one place, and never more than ten shots with any one club. And try different shots in these routines. Flops over bunkers. Bump-and-runs onto greens. Fly the ball to the pin, and then drop a wedge onto the putting surface and have it release. Raymond Floyd is a member of Shinnecock and also Seminole, and I watched him work this way at both places. And if it's good enough for Raymond . . .

Another thing I like to do is have one of my students stand 20 yards or so off the green and hit three different clubs to the same spot. A 9-iron, say, as well as a pitching wedge and then their primary sand wedge. Harvey

Druga says that one way to make your practice sessions effective is to pick targets for every shot you hit on the range.

Penick used to do something similar with Ben Crenshaw and Tom Kite. He'd send them over to the practice green and get them to flip 9-irons over a bunker onto a green as well as sand wedges. It not only builds proficiency in that all-important aspect of the game but also versatility. I believe it fosters confidence as well and gives you that sense that you can create and manufacture shots if need be when you are playing an actual round.

Then there is putting, and I start with the thought that I want guys to practice with some sort of pressure, with a game. I love what Phil Mickelson does, which is put four tees around a golf hole so that he has putts from four different angles. And he has to make them all in order to move onto the next hole. You put pressure on yourself to do that, and that pressure builds as you get to the third and fourth putt.

As a rule, I think it is best to practice putts in the three- to six-foot range, as those are the real difference makers when it comes to scoring. But it is also critical to practice those very long putts, the 50- or 60-footers that no one seems to work on.

The matter of preround putting comes up often, and I find that abbreviated versions of those putting games work for most people. But sometimes it is just enough to get the speed of the green right and not worry about putting golf balls into the holes. Jack Nicklaus once told me he never practiced to a hole on tournament days because he didn't want to be worried about missing a couple of three-footers before he went off to the first tee. That was the last thing he wanted on his mind as he got ready to play. So he would just putt to spots.

Pressure often comes into play when we putt. So Druga recommends putting pressure on yourself when you practice with your flat stick by playing games in which you have to make different-length putts from different angles.

Jack Druga is the head professional at the Shinnecock Hills Golf Club in Southampton, New York, site of the 2018 US Open. A former assistant pro at Oakmont Country Club and Seminole Golf Club, he also served for 11 years as the head professional of the Country Club of Fairfield in Fairfield, Connecticut. Druga has distinguished himself in several aspects of the game over the years, having won the Met PGA's Bill Strausbaugh Award for Employment Contributions in 2001 and the section's Merchandiser of the Year award in 2010. In 2009, Druga won the Met PGA Senior Championship and two years later captured the Long Island Senior Open Championship.

# CHAPTER FOUR

# Putting

## Mike Shannon, Sea Island Golf Club

Here's the thing about putting that most golfers do not understand: every one of us has the ability to putt as well as a tour professional. No fooling. It's the one aspect of the game where there is no physical barrier. It's not like we have to be as big and strong and flexible as a pro to hit a drive 300 yards. But you and I can have 26 putts in a round on any given day. We can be as good as anybody on tour.

Mike Shannon, Sea Island Golf Club. Courtesy of Sea Island Golf Club.

Of course, if we want to putt as well as a tour professional, then we have to do the same things he does to make that happen. For starters, all great putters on tour have the ability to aim the putter correctly. Aim is a product of vision, dominant eye, and eye triangulation for an individual player and finding the ball position that suits his eyes best and optimizes his putting performance. He can figure that out through a bit of trial and error, and once he determines his optimal ball position on his putts, he will be able to aim the ball properly each and every time. My advice is to work with your PGA golf professional to determine whether your ball position is correct. If it's too far forward, he will be able to see that you are aiming to the left of your target (as a right-handed player). And if it is too far back, it will be evident that you are aiming to the right. Once you find the best ball position for you, then you should have tour-quality aim.

Getting in a good address position is important, too, and I have determined there are four critical lines in that regard. The first is the line you form from the ball to the cup. Then there is the "eye line," where the eyes have to be square, or parallel, to the intended line of the putt. The "shoulder line" should also be parallel to that line, as well as the "elbow and forearm line." Believe it or not, the position of the feet has nothing to do with direction. Some touring pros will be open with their stance, and others will be closed. But the one thing they all have in common is the eyes, shoulders, elbows, and forearms being parallel to the intended line.

Another thing the best putters do successfully is eliminate excessive motion from their putting strokes. And the best strokes come from use of the big muscles of the body, the upper back, shoulders, and upper chest, and not the arms or hands. If you use your arms and hands with your putting, then you are creating excess motion.

Mechanically, those are the things the best putters do so well, and if you can do them yourself, you can greatly improve your putting. But for the best, mechanics is only about 20 percent of why they are so successful. The rest comes from their speed and distance control as well as visualization and the ability to read greens. And figuring out those things is what is really going to take you, as a putter, to the next level.

I fervently believe that players have a certain speed that allows them to maximize their putting results. Tiger Woods has always been a very aggressive putter, and he looks to hit a ball three or four feet past the hole. Brad Faxon, on the other hand, prefers to drop his putts in just over the front edge. He likes to die them in the hole. Both are very good putters, yet they could not be more different as far as their speeds are concerned. If they chose to switch speeds and imitate the way the other putts, then they would not have nearly as much success.

Every person has his or her own speed, the one that works for that individual game, and figuring that out and being consistent with it is a key to good putting. It will help you make more putts, and the more consistent your speed, the easier it will be to read the greens. I encourage my students to pay attention to putts they hit during a round or on a practice green from six feet, ten feet, and then 12 feet. See how far past the hole you hit your putts or how short you come up, and work off of that information to develop a speed that best suits you and your eye. Get to know that speed, and work off of that going forward.

I have a drill I use all the time to help golfers develop consistent putting speed. Take a cart towel, and lay it about 12 inches behind the cup. Then start hitting putts from three feet away, and work your way all the way to 30-footers, in three-foot increments. And strive to make every putt either stop in the cup or on the towel behind the cup. Make it a game, and every time you miss the towel, either from being too long or too short, you have to start over. Don't think about mechanics in this drill, just think about speed, and it will help develop one that is consistent and very much your own.

Mike Shannon is the putting instructor for the Sea Island Learning Center at the Sea Island Golf Club on St. Simons Island, Georgia. Both *Golf Digest* and *Golf* magazine have named him among the top instructors in the country, and Shannon is a three-time PGA section Teacher of the Year. He has worked with more than 150 players from the PGA, LPGA, Champions, and European PGA Tours, and currently counts Matt Kuchar, Jeff Overton, Heath Slocum, and Shaun Micheel among his students.

# CHAPTER FIVE

# How to Better Compete

## Darrell Kestner, Deepdale Golf Club

It is important to begin any discussion on competing with a simple premise: we compete as golfers because we love competition. We are doing it to have fun, whether it is an elite amateur or professional tournament, a simple member-guest or a charity scramble. Whatever the event, we need to be sure to have fun.

Darrell Kestner holding the trophy after winning the PGA Club Professional Championship in 1996.

In my playing career to date, I tried to qualify for 25 US Opens—and made it to eight of them. The first few times I tried, I felt so nervous and let myself get frustrated by bad shots. I took on so much stress that I never played very well, certainly not well enough to make it to the Open. Then, I decided just to go out and have fun. As soon as I did that, I managed to qualify, and I found over the years that every time I approached the qualifying tournaments for the Open with that attitude, I made it in.

It is especially important for the club player to try and have fun whenever he competes, because he is not built or conditioned to take on a lot of stress. Generally speaking, neither his game nor his mind is strong enough for that, because he does not regularly compete. He does not have the experience, and as a result, his game breaks down far too easily under pressure. Consequently, he is going to have a very difficult time doing well under those conditions. The game is hard enough as it is, so the best thing he can do is enjoy the experience and not let the pressure get to him too much.

To be sure, we are all going to feel pressure when we play tournaments. The key is embracing the pressure when it comes and seeing it as something that is part of the fun of competing.

Another thing golfers have to guard against is letting their emotions get the better of them. One of the most important attributes of a great competitor is his or her ability to overcome adversity, to rise above a bad bounce, a bad shot, or bad weather. I remember watching Jason Dufner in a tournament during the 2012 PGA Tour season birdie one hole and then double bogey the next and eagle the one after that. And I never saw the expression on his face change. Not once. When I play in tournaments, I try not to get too excited either way, either. I do not get too pumped over a great shot or too down over a bad one. I try to think of Ben Hogan, who often said that the most important shot is the next one. I make it a point not to get too upset because I know even the very best players in the world make mistakes. That way, I can maintain my focus on the task at hand, which is putting the ball in the cup with as few strokes as possible and recovering as quickly as possible from the mistakes I make.

It is critical to competitive success on the golf course that a player know what it is to be a golfer. I think of that point often because I am in my late 50s now, and I go up against kids all the time who are driving the ball 50 yards past me. I have to remind myself that if golf was all about distance, then the long drivers would be winning everything on the PGA Tour. But they are not. The actual key to success is being able to post a number or win a match, to hit greens in regulation with longer irons and hybrids, to have a short game that can make up for a lack of distance or an inability to hit greens in regulation each and every time, to have the skills to get creative with shot making and be able to hit a variety of shots when they come up on the course.

For club players, it is also critical that they play their own games in competition. Don't get intimidated by the big hitter and try to keep up with him. Don't be impressed by an opponent who draws the ball beautifully and try to do that yourself, even though your natural shot is a fade. Only worry about the shots you have to play, and play them the way you know best, being sure to enjoy the challenge of it all.

I touched earlier on the importance for club players of being able to hit different shots, and it reminds me of how invaluable it can be to practice those shots as well. It is fine to work on your mid-iron play on the range or to hit a bunch of drives. But be sure to work on other aspects of your game, too. Balls out of fairway bunkers. Flop shots over greenside bunkers. Try a few long irons off of sidehill lies. Put a couple of golf balls in divots to see how you do with those. Change your targets. Work on hitting those hybrids off of green collars. The more you can prepare yourself for the types of shots that inevitably come up during a tournament round and be somewhat comfortable hitting them, the better you can stay calm and focused when you need to make them, especially as a club player, for even the very best club players are not hitting all their shots in competition from perfect, practice range–like lies in the middle of the fairway.

While we are on the subject of practice, I am compelled to reiterate the importance of working on your short game. Go to a PGA Tour event and hang around the practice area for a while, and you will see that as a rule, touring pros spend about 75 percent of their time at the short-game areas. Good as he is with his driver, you rarely see Bubba Watson hitting that club on tour ranges. He always seems to be chipping and putting. Same with Phil Mickelson and Luke Donald. They know they can save strokes, and save tournaments, by being extra strong with their short games, and club players should recognize that, too. It's an especially big factor in those match play events they enter all the time, for so many holes are won and lost on the basis of whether one player can get up and down. In addition, nothing discourages an opponent quite so much as your being able to find ways to make pars from all around the green. You break down a competitor's resolve and really mess up his focus when you do that.

Being proficient in those areas is really about being a golfer, and if you are going to compete with any success at whatever level is right for you, you need to understand that. You need to go beyond basic ball striking. Learn to get the ball into the hole. Learn to hit all the different shots. Learn to adjust your mental approach on the course and also to understand swing and shot fundamentals enough to diagnose problems when they come up during a round and then correct them—things such as aim, balance, and tempo. Stance, grip, and alignment, too. I like to give lessons on becoming that golfer, and time spent on developing that aspect of your game can pay big dividends when you tee it up in a tournament.

I have also found in tournaments that I do best when I make a good plan and prepare myself properly for the competition. That entails practice, of course, but also stretching and working out. Nutrition. Sleep. It may sound strange, but sleep is so important when it comes to competing at your very best because it is impossible to focus properly and be strong physically if you are tired from not enough sleep.

I learned the hard way about making a good plan at the first major championships in which I competed. I worked so hard in the days leading up to them that I had no energy by the time the tournament started. The touring professionals do their homework well in advance of an event and are sure they are fresh when it is time to play.

I remember in 1996, when I won the National Club Pro Championship, I took a completely different tack. Instead of practicing hard, I backed way off. I hit maybe a bucket of balls each day. I putted for maybe five minutes. Then I went back to the hotel room and rested. I felt so fresh and so relaxed that I ended up winning the tournament.

Making that plan will help a club player, too. So will remembering that I also helped myself in that tournament by making sure I had fun. And I played very well as a result.

Darrell Kestner is one of the most accomplished PGA club professionals of his generation when it comes to competitive play. He has won the Met Open Championship three times, the Westchester PGA and New York State Open twice each, and the Met PGA Championship five times. Kestner has also qualified for eight US Opens, ten PGA Championships, two US Senior Opens, and seven PGA Senior Championships. The PGA of America has twice named him National Senior Player of the Year, and he has been honored several times for his teaching as well.

# CHAPTER SIX

# Club Fitting

## Brendan Walsh, The Country Club

Brendan Walsh, The Country Club

There are three primary ways a person can improve as a golfer these days. One is through instruction, and another is by building strength and increasing flexibility through exercise. Then there is club fitting, which can not only make the game a lot easier but also more fun.

Playing with equipment that does not fit is unhelpful on a couple of levels. For one thing, it is much harder to play well and hit the ball properly if you are using clubs that are too long or short, too heavy or light, or too stiff or flexible. Often, ill-fitting equipment will force you to make adjustments and compensations with your swing that not only destroy your basic mechanics but also cause injury.

As a teaching professional, there is nothing I enjoy more than seeing results when my students play and practice. And there are few things as gratifying as taking someone who has been using the wrong equipment and putting them into clubs that fit. The results are simply staggering, and my students have a real "Wow!" moment when they see what a difference properly fit equipment makes. I watch men and women golfers gain 10 to 20 yards in distance alone simply by getting them into, say, a driver that is better suited for them in terms of loft, shaft flex, and length, and they could not be more pleased.

That is why club fitting is so important. At The Country Club, where I work and teach, the majority of our members have been fit because we have long offered that service, and they are so good about buying from the pro. But I would say that overall in golf, only about 30 percent of those who play with any regularity are fit, which means there is a vast segment of the golfing populace who have yet to take advantage of this option.

And it really is a terrific option. All the major equipment manufacturers offer club fitting, and their company websites give detailed information on where you may get fit if your PGA professional cannot fit you. Most green-grass and off-course professionals as well as the majority of fitting centers feature more than one brand, too, so your options are great. Some companies even have tour vans that travel the country, going to clubs and courses to give players the same service that club makers provide their touring professionals, which is the ultimate in customization. It is possible to get fit indoors or outdoors, although I always prefer having it done outdoors, where the fitter has the opportunity to watch ball flight. Even with all the high-tech equipment in the world, you still need the human eye element to it. To be sure, the process can be a bit time consuming, and yes, a new set of irons or metals costs money. But the investment is so worth it, especially if you are looking to play your best possible golf.

Typically, the first thing I do in a fitting is interview the golfer to get a sense of the clubs he or she currently uses as I also learn about his golf game, the way he plays, the things he does well, and what he wants to improve on. Then I have him hit his 6-iron, which most equipment companies believe is the club that gives the best fitting data, as it is right between being a long and short iron. We put tape on the sole and clubface so that I can learn what the proper lie angle and club length are and where the golfer is hitting the ball on the clubface. It's a way of seeing how well or poorly his current set of clubs fits and where we need to go to make his new set fit properly.

Once we start to figure that out, it is time to introduce shafts. At that point, I am getting a good feel for his swings and swing tendencies. And with the ways we can now switch shafts and clubheads so easily, we can try a variety of shafts to see how he hits each one. What I want to do is put him in the lightest shaft possible, unless I am dealing with a golfer with a very high swing speed. No matter the player, though, I am always looking for the combination of clubs and shafts that gives him or her optimal ball flight, optimal launch conditions, and optimal spin.

While we are on the subject of shafts, it is a good time to note that there are both ones made of steel and ones made of graphite. Typically, steel shafts have a bit more consistency than graphite, and until recently they were usually heavier. Most touring pros employ steel shafts in their irons because their games are so precise, and they really need that consistency. But all the steel shaft makers are now producing steel shafts that are considerably lighter than their predecessors, which gives recreational players even more shaft options, though they tend to find graphite works best for them in their iron mixes. As a rule, the pros all use graphite in their drivers, and most of them have graphite in their fairway metals and hybrids, too.

Once we get the irons set, we start working on the driver, where we want to get the best possible angle at launch to maximize distance, looking for more of an ascending blow that gets the ball up in the air.

Then we move onto fairways and hybrids. Part of our work here has to do with gapping, figuring out how far a player hits each of those clubs and how well he hits them. Then it is a question of where we want the bigger gaps. There is no set rule here; rather, we work with individual golfers and see what works best for them. Generally speaking, we want the gaps to be smaller with the shorter irons, the wedges, because that is where the greatest precision is required, and larger with hybrids and fairway metals, where choking up and down can easily vary distances. We do a lot of work when fitting wedges and putters, and that usually necessitates a separate visit. But that is time well spent, for those are the scoring clubs. With wedges, we want to see how far a golfer hits wedges of different degrees, from the pitching wedges at 48 degrees to lob wedges at 60. We also want to discern what the best bounce for a golfer is. Is he a digger? Does he have a steep angle of attack? If so, we want to give him as much bounce as possible with his wedges. If he comes at a ball in a shallower way, then less bounce. Looking at the depth of the divot he makes is critical to determining how much bounce to give him. Also, understanding where he plays most of his golf is a factor, too. Typically, firmer turf means you need less bounce, while you want more with softer ground.

These are the sorts of things fitters get into with their golfers, and it can make all the difference with the way they play the game. It's the same with putters, and it matters not only how long or short a putter is for individual players but also the way it is balanced and how it is shafted, whether in the heel, for example, or in the center of the putter head. The path of your putting stroke can make a difference as well.

The best players in the world have been fitted for years. Now that option is just as available to recreational golfers. If you love the game and want to play up to your fullest capabilities, then you should be sure to get properly fit.

Brendan Walsh has been the head golf professional at The Country Club in Brookline, Massachusetts, since 1998. Prior to going to work at that prestigious retreat, Walsh served as the head golf professional at the Patterson Club in Fairfield, Connecticut, home club of PGA touring professional J. J. Henry. In addition to being an acclaimed teacher, Walsh is also an accomplished player, and in 1996 he captured the Connecticut Open.

# CHAPTER SEVEN

# Finding Five

## Scott Nye, Merion Golf Club

Merion head golf professional
Scott Nye

The challenge for any golf instructor goes beyond teaching basic swing techniques and the ways a player hits the different clubs in his bag. It also entails helping him improve his scores—and helping move his game in the right direction in that regard. I am talking about another way for a golfer to get better, and it involves making an honest assessment of the strengths and weaknesses of his game and also the development of a road map he can follow to lower his scores and handicap indexes and enhance his enjoyment of the sport.

In many ways, golf can be so discouraging for players because they get to a point where they do not believe they can get better. They do not see the potential they can reach. They do not believe there is a way to lower their scores with reasonable ease. And as a result, they often give up.

But I have come up with a way to help my students get better and rekindle their passion for the game as well as their beliefs that they can indeed improve their scores as they also enjoy the sport. It all revolves around something I call "finding five." As in five strokes they can shave off their games, using nine-holes scores in descending order from 50 to 35 as benchmarks. And I keep working with them as their scores drop, figuring out at each five-shot interval how they can shed even more.

How do I do this? I start by understanding where they are with their games. How well do they play? How often do they tee it up, and how frequently do they practice? I then ask them what they want from golf, whether they plan to play competitively, and how much they really want to get better. I also need to find out at this point whether they are willing to take the necessary steps to get better.

Then I get into assessing their games, the things they do well and not so well. I develop a custom list for each one, and we go from there.

I can do any number of things to help a player find five strokes based on that information, and that is my job from that point forward. And as I teach them the ways to find five, I also try to educate them on how to coach themselves, to find the things they can do to shed those five strokes on their own as well as with my assistance.

Not surprisingly, the process differs for individual players, depending on their skill levels and the things on which they need to work. For example, what does a player who shoots 50 for nine holes need to do to get down to

Finding five is all about finding ways to shave five strokes off your score. To help his students find five, Nye customizes a list with each one of how they can best achieve that.

45? One thing is to make a few more putts, so we will do some work on that. More accurate chipping and pitching is important, too, because a player with that high a handicap is not likely getting on greens in regulation—and is very likely mishitting chips and pitches around a green. Keeping the ball in play is critical, too, and it is a good idea to introduce the concept of course management and the many things a golfer can do to cut down on the kinds of mental mistakes that can kill a round. Maybe it is emphasizing the importance of staying below the hole when he chips and pitches. Maybe it is stressing the need to go for the center of the green on an approach and ignore the pin when it is tucked in a difficult spot. I also talk a lot about the short game and the importance of "finishing" the last 25 yards of every hole—and understanding just how they do that. It's a rudimentary start, but it is one that gives a golfer a way to get rid of those five strokes. And in a very practical way.

For those who really want to master the game, I work my way down to scoring 35 for nine holes by devising different things a player can do to "find five," in five-stroke increments. Of course, it gets more difficult to shave those strokes the farther you go toward 35. But there are things we can do the whole way down to make it happen.

I think it's fair to say a golfer can apply many of the same approaches as he looks to go from 45 to 40 as he did to go from 50 to 45. Improve putting. Improve chipping and pitching. Get better at course management. Again, it can vary greatly from player to player, depending on their strengths and weaknesses, and I recommend you take this approach to your own PGA club professional for his input on how you can make it happen.

Now, going from 40 to 35 can be very difficult as well, and it may well take as long as a year of solid play and practice to accomplish. But it can be done with competitive practice, refined technique that comes with additional lessons, increased distance off the tee and accuracy on approach shots, and better chipping, pitching, and putting. Again, find the best ways to take five strokes off your games.

I have a junior player with whom I have worked a lot, and I remember his playing in a tournament and shooting 95 the first day and 87 the next. He was not happy, and we chatted on the phone afterward. We went over his round and determined that he posted four double bogeys the first day and two the second. We discussed that if he had simply made bogey each time during those six holes instead of double he would have saved six shots. If he had managed a couple of pars, he could have cut eight strokes off for each day. Most of those doubles we determined were the result of three-putts, so we then knew there was one aspect of the game on which he could focus his practice going forward. What had been a distressing experience for the player turned out to be one we could build on, and he did much better the next tournament he played.

It is a good exercise for all of us to go through, and it can really make a difference in the ways we play. Most people I know want full-swing lessons,

To improve a player's short game, Nye likes to drop three balls at different spots 100 yards and closer to the green and then have the player complete the hole with each one, with three being par.

and they figure learning those techniques will help them get better. To be sure, that helps. But many times, a player will benefit more by concentrating on how to score from inside 25 yards of the hole. It's the precision, the refinement they need on all sorts of shots around the green that will help them save strokes and find five. It's putting and course management, knowing which parts of the fairway to hit with their drives and which quadrants on the green they need to reach with their approaches.

I remember some years ago getting ready to play in a sectional championship and spending time at my home club at Merion working on my iron play beforehand. I hit four balls on a few holes in a row onto the green, all inside 160 yards and all from different places and distances. And I discovered that my tendency was to come up short. I knew that I needed to get my approaches closer if I was going to do well in the tournament, so I decided to take one extra club each time when it came time to compete, to make sure I did that. And it made a difference.

Another game I play with my students as I help them try to find five is to take three golf balls with us out to the course. We get within 25 or 30 yards of the green, and I put all three balls down on the ground, in three different places. Then I ask my student to complete the hole with all three balls. We look at par as being three strokes per ball, and the goal is to get them to figure out and work on the best ways for them to put each ball in the hole and to save strokes doing so. As we progress, as the student gets better at the game, we go back to 50 or 60 yards, then to 100 yards, and maybe all the way to 140 or 150, all the while learning how to get down in three strokes or less.

It's a way for them to get better and better—to learn how to manage their games, and to find ways to "find five."

Scott Nye has been the head professional at the Merion Golf Club in Ardmore, Pennsylvania, since 2000. During his tenure, the club has hosted the US Amateur and the Walker Cup as well as the US Open. Previously, he served as head professional at the Country Club of York in Pennsylvania. Nye is a two-time winner of the Philadelphia PGA's Horton Smith Award, given for outstanding contributions to professional education, and was a four-time All-American at the College of Wooster.

# CHAPTER EIGHT

# Iron and Hybrid Play

## Eden Foster, Maidstone Club

There is so much emphasis on driving and putting when it comes to talk about golf instruction and how they are the most important shots to master. That's understandable, but it is just as critical for players to know how to hit their irons and hybrids properly. And it makes sense to cover both irons and hybrids in the same chapter, as they should be hit in much the same way.

Eden Foster, Maidstone Club

41

Let's start with hybrids, which have become very important pieces of equipment for recreational golfers because they are so easy to hit and can be used in any number of different situations. Off the tee or off the deck on the fairway. Out of the rough and out of divots. Off of hardpan lies, too. You can hit them high or low, and it is not that hard to work the ball with a hybrid, hitting fades or draws if need be. Then, of course, you can employ those clubs around the green, when a shot has settled on the collar, for example, or stopped shot of the putting surface. They really are something else, and I am steering more and more of my students away from the long irons, the 3- and 4-iron and even the 5-iron, and into hybrids. Hybrids are not only easier to hit, as I have already mentioned. But long irons are getting harder, as the lofts of modern ones are made stronger through the set. People also have a tendency to try and help the ball into the air when they use long irons, and when they do that, they get "backwards shaft lean" and consequently hit the ball heavy or thin.

For the purposes of this chapter, we are going to talk about hitting hybrids off of fairways and out of the rough, as you would an iron, in an effort to put your approach shots on the green. And the first thing we should discuss is the misconception golfers often have that they should hit their hybrids in a sweeping way, as they would a fairway metal. I feel it is better to hit hybrids with a descending blow, trapping the golf ball as you would with an iron. Use a sweeping swing with a hybrid, and chances are you will hit the golf ball with the bottom of the clubhead. You will tend to top it.

Keep in mind that the better player likes to trap the ball—with every shot, for the most part, but the drive. Trapping creates backspin, which creates lift, which then results in distance. A sweeping swing puts topspin on the ball, and it will not travel in the air as much (though it will run out on the ground).

Proper ball position is also a consideration with hybrids, and generally speaking, you want to position the ball a bit farther back in your stance than you would a fairway metal. The ball flight might be a tad lower than expected, but the contact will be much better.

I like to see my students use more of a descending blow with their irons. To be fair, a good player will put more of a sweeping swing on, say, a 3-iron than he will a 7-iron. But he or she is still hitting in a downward motion, and that is important to remember.

One drill I use a lot to help develop that type of swing with iron play is what I call the punch shot drill. And when I explain it to my members, I tell them to think in terms of tennis. If you want to put a lot of topspin on the ball, you finish high. But if you are looking to hit backspin, you finish low, with your ground strokes and also your volleys. Well, an iron shot is like a volley. So is a punch shot, with a low finish below the chest, with a descending blow on the ball. I like my students to get a feel for that low finish and that downward swing motion by punching a series of shots with, say, their 6-iron. At first, I want them to finish with the club below the chest or shoulders. But as they feel they are hitting downward on the ball properly, then they can complete a fuller swing and finish with a fuller follow-through.

My members ask me all the time about the best way to play par-3s, and how they can hit the best possible shot on those holes and get their tee shots on the green. It's invariably an important part of the round for them, as recreational golfers see par-3s as holes when they should be able to score, where they at the very least should make a par and also have a chance at a birdie. One thing I've noticed is how many recreational players tee up their golf balls too high. They may have 140 yards, which would normally be a perfect 8-iron shot. But then they tee up the ball too high and seem surprised when it comes up ten yards short. They are inadvertently adding loft to their irons when they tee up their golf balls too high, which means that in the case of the 8-iron, it becomes a 9. Also, they tend to stroke the ball higher on the clubface when it is teed up, which takes away distance as well because it is above the sweet spot. Be conscious, then, of teeing up the ball too high. And if you like it that way, be sure to compensate by taking more club.

While we are on the subject of teeing up iron shots, I cannot help but think how so many of my teaching professional peers did what I used to do when I gave lessons to beginners, and that was to tee up the ball for them to help them hit the ball and enjoy some early successes. But it is the worst possible thing you can do, for it encourages that sweeping motion and that backward shaft lean that come from trying to get the ball in the air. What I've found is that it is far better to use artificial turf mats so that students can learn to hit down on the ball without the worry of sticking the club into the ground. Those mats are so forgiving, and they give such positive feedback to a new player as they teach him or her to swing irons in the proper way.

Eden Foster is the head professional at the Maidstone Club in East Hampton, New York. He is among *Golf* magazine's top 100 instructors in the United States.

# CHAPTER NINE

# How to Take an Efficient Lesson

## Suzy Whaley, TPC at River Highlands

Most golfers probably agree that lessons by and large are good for them. It's how they learn new things about their swings and the ways they play the game. It's also a way to reaffirm techniques and approaches they've absorbed in previous sessions.

Problem is, not everyone knows that there are good and bad ways to take lessons and for

The Connecticut PGA Section has named Suzy Whaley its teacher of the year twice. Courtesy of Montana Pritchard, PGA of America.

instructors to give them. My hope here is to make the process of working with a PGA teaching professional as effective and efficient as possible.

For starters, I think it is helpful for students to understand how we as PGA teaching professionals think and operate as we approach the lesson process. My methodology revolves around my desire to help my students lower their scores. I evaluate and instruct each student based on his or her own personal goals and ability levels. I do not advocate a particular theory but instead teach them how to change current behavior into successful behaviors. My goal is to help students realize the area where the most shots can be shaved from their usual scores, and I show them how to make that weakness a strength. All students get better when they are trained to practice correctly for improvement.

At the same time, I think it is important to balance my students' joy for their games by not focusing all the time on numbers. To be sure, lowering scores does come from things such as technique changes. But it also is a result of students understanding and appreciating all that golf offers and enjoying their time on the course and also the range.

As far as the motion of the swing, I believe the swing is more about swinging the club than hitting at the golf ball. When you swing the clubhead, it moves the hands, arms, and shoulders, and the big muscles like the chest and legs follow, reacting to and supporting the effort. The weight of the clubhead hinges the wrists and the lower body reacts, transferring the weight, keeping the clubhead on the target line through the impact area, assuring a more consistent ball flight through a square clubface at impact. Impact in the golf swing is crucial, and students need to be aware of what causes errant shots. I believe in teaching my students ball flight laws and how to correct their mistakes based on those laws. When my students can

As any golfer gets ready to start instruction with a PGA professional, tell him or her why you are seeking help and describe what immediate and long-term goals you have. Courtesy of Montana Pritchard, PGA of America.

self-correct based on ball flight laws, their time spent on the golf course is more enjoyable and results in lower scores.

When analyzing a student's performance, I evaluate athleticism, balance, attitude, and enjoyment. Athleticism tells me a student's ability to improve quickly and allows me to use sports analogies. Balance is crucial to a student's ability to swing correctly. If balance and flexibility are not present, I adjust expectations and teach to reality for a good golf outcome. Attitude tells me a lot about a student's pleasure and commitment to the game. Their enjoyment of the learning process and curiosity tells me how they acquire skills and their passion to play and improve. I believe in empowering my students with knowledge and self-awareness to self-correct so that they can measure and work toward continual improvement. I also find that the students who play more golf and find joy in the pursuit of their next shots are those I have reached most deeply as a coach.

Finally, I believe that instruction takes patience, kindness, positive reinforcement, shaping steps, and the ability to keep students at ease. A student who trusts you and is comfortable with the steps you are introducing will learn faster. You must love teaching to become a great instructor. I strive every day to get better and continue to learn to help my students change behavior and improve their performance.

I have a couple of lists to share, the first of which represents the student perspective to taking efficient and effective lessons and what he or she can do with regard to that. And I believe it is well worth considering when you start working with a PGA teaching professional yourself:

1. Begin by laying out your background in golf, including how you score; what injuries, if any, you might have; your physical and mental strengths

Everyone likes to hit a driver, but you will be best served if you devote 80 percent of your lesson time working on your short game. That's what will improve your score most dramatically. Courtesy of Montana Pritchard, PGA of America.

and weaknesses; and the amount of time you have to play. Be specific as to what the hole in your game might be and where you want to improve. Be honest, too, as to what needs work and what does not. Let your teacher know about anything that may keep you from reaching your goals. A bum knee, perhaps. An absolute aversion to hitting balls out of bunkers. Also, ask about rates.

2. Then explain to your professional why you are seeking his or her help and what immediate goals you might have. It is also a good time to lay out why you have chosen that person to help you.

3. Look at the long term for a moment, and let the professional know what your ultimate goals in golf are.

4. I recommend you bring a notepad and pen in a plastic ziplock bag to each lesson so that you may take proper notes and keep track of techniques you learn and suggestions your professional is making. You can also use an iPhone or Android for this. Data collecting is critical to absorbing information you receive from your teacher and using it to improve. It is also helpful for monitoring progress. Take advantage of teaching moments that arise during the lessons.

5. Develop an attitude that you hope and expect to improve. Commit to being an active part of the learning process, and be patient in learning new steps for advancement.

6. Choose an instructor who commits to changing behavior through self-awareness and one who observes areas of opportunity for reaching goals and then focuses the student in those areas. Do plenty of research to find the teacher best suited for you.

7. Perform each change at a slow rate of speed until mastered. Understand that progress can take time. Manage expectations and be realistic as to how quickly you will progress.

8. Choose an instructor who gives positive reinforcement and helps you self-correct so that you can own the skill and repeat it on the course. It is also imperative to find a teacher who has your goals at the forefront of each lesson and is as committed to helping you as you are to getting help.

9. Devote 80 percent of your lesson time to working on your short game. Use the other 20 percent for long-game instruction. Yes, the short game really is that important.

10. At the same time, make a point of learning practice skills that simulate course skills and then working on them as much as possible. Work out a series of drills with your instructor to work on outside of your lessons together.

11. Find a teacher who incorporates on-course instruction as well as lessons on rules and etiquette.

As for the second list, it covers what the golf instructor needs to do to give efficient lessons, and it is a good thing not only for professionals to consider but also golfers looking to find the best possible teacher. And students should be discriminating about who they choose, as they will no doubt be spending lots of time and money trying to get better. So why not know all they can to make sure that happens?

1. An instructor should be positive, energetic, and upbeat to the student, regardless of conditions or the player's ability. She should be sure to tell students she is there for them and that she will continue to help them progress. She should be clear on what the students' goals are and what they should hope to achieve.

2. A teacher should describe her expectations for the lesson and debunk common myths of instruction and appreciate the students' actions of coming to her with seriousness and being committed to their improvement.

3. I recommend that teaching professionals take a personal interest in their students' stories and their journeys in golf. Get to know and appreciate their backgrounds to better understand their areas of opportunity and interest.

4. Measure performance to design performance standards and feedback for improvement. Manage expectations. Communicate behavior and practice techniques for positive results. Work to lower the anxiety and fear levels of your students.

5. Be clear and specific in changes expected throughout the lesson process, and have students take notes for future reference. Give specific practice goals and exercises to reinforce improvement with data tracking.

6. Introduce changes and new techniques gradually to allow the students to adjust to new positions at their own pace and after repetitive motion that is guided by the instructor.

7. Understand that self-feedback is critical to improvement, as is data collection, so that students can understand areas to focus on for achieving their goals.

8. Teach far more short-game lessons.

9. Offer tips on books and magazines to read, and share thoughts on equipment options. It is also important to discuss fitness, nutrition, and conditioning.

Suzy Whaley is a PGA and LPGA golf clinician at TPC River Highlands in Cromwell, Connecticut. A graduate of the University of North Carolina, where she played on the golf team for four years and graduated with a BS degree in economics, she played for two years on the LPGA Tour. In July 2003, Whaley became the first woman to qualify for and participate in a PGA Tour event since the legendary Babe Zaharias did so 58 years earlier. Whaley has been recognized as a top teacher in the state of Connecticut by *Golf Digest* and is a district 1 director of the PGA board of directors. The Connecticut PGA section has named her Teacher of the Year twice, and in 2003 she won its Bill Strausbaugh Award.

# CHAPTER TEN

# Chipping

## Gene Mattare, Saucon Valley Country Club

One of the first questions golfers have about chipping is: When should I do it? A good rule of thumb is "putt when you can, and chip when you can't putt." That speaks to the simple truth that a ball traveling along the ground is easier to control than one traveling in the air. But chips don't get very high in the air at

Gene Mattare of the Saucon Valley Country Club asks his players to go through a quick checklist as they get ready to hit their chips.

all. At least they shouldn't, which means they are not that difficult to make and master.

Generally speaking, the chip is a one-lever swing used from just off the putting surface. The desired shot involves maximum "ground time" and minimum "air time." It is easier to judge the roll of a ball than it is to determine distance through the air.

There are two primary methods of chipping: the traditional, or classic, technique and the "Runyan" method, named after the great teacher and touring professional Paul Runyan. Both can be very effective, and with some practice, you should be able to determine which style works best for you.

So what club should you use? I prefer to chip with a variety of clubs, depending on conditions, but you may find one that you are comfortable with and use that exclusively. Either is fine. The pitching wedge, sand wedge, 9-, 8-, and 7-iron are the chipping clubs of choice for most golfers.

As for the grip, you may opt for the one you use for putting or the one you employ for all other shots, a normal grip that is overlapping or interlocking. Whatever you select, be sure to use the one that best enables you to reduce—if not eliminate—"wristinesss" in the stroke. And don't forget the virtues of "choking down" for better control and feel.

Now it is time to discuss setup. As with any shot in golf, you must have a good preshot routine and setup. And I recommend you go through the following checklist: examine the lie, analyze the shot you are going to play, approach the ball from behind, set the clubface to the target, assume an address position with the feet and hips slightly "open," use light grip pressure, and play the ball in the center of a narrow stance while favoring your weight slightly on the left side.

All of these clubs can be used to hit chips. It all depends on which ones you are most comfortable with and the type of shot you want to hit.

In the address position, the feet and hips should be set to the left of the target or "open," which makes it easier to see and swing toward the spot you have picked out. It also forces the backswing to remain on line longer and restricts the length of the backswing for better control.

The arms should hang comfortably from the shoulders, not reaching or crowding, while the hands should hang about a fist's width from the left

of the full swing. Chipping incorporates the correct swing path and clubface angle, the correct position of the left wrist at impact, and the relationship between the clubhead, hands, and body through the hitting area at the full swing. And training yourself to repeat a simple chipping action with correct fundamentals is the best way to correct major faults in your full swing.

I have a few drills that will assist you in your short-game practice, beginning with the one I call "develop a formula for different clubs." The purpose of this is to help you accurately judge how far the ball carries and rolls with clubs of different lofts, and the procedure is as follows: using a pitching wedge, sand wedge, 9-, 8-, and 7-irons, find a level area and hit a few chip shots with each club. Employ the same chipping motion with each club, and see how far each ball carries and rolls. Once you develop a feel for what each club is capable of doing, you will be better able to transfer this knowledge to various situations on the course.

Next is the "circle drill," and the purpose of that is to provide a picture of where to land the ball to obtain the desired result. Start by picking out a target on the green, and through trial and error find a spot on the green where the ball must land in order to roll close to the hole. Lay some string or a tee or merely visualize a six-foot circle around the spot. Practice landing your shots anywhere within the circle, and let the ball roll near the hole. This emphasizes that it is not necessary to have pinpoint accuracy to obtain a good result.

You may also want to try the "parallel club drill," which is designed to help keep shots on line and provide a visual cue for a good takeaway and follow-through. It also teaches clubface control, correct swing path, and proper angle of attack. To do this drill, lay two clubs parallel to each other aimed at the hole or area of the putting green you are hitting toward. Using a

7-iron, practice making a perfect chipping stroke with the clubhead traveling only slightly inside the line of play on the backswing and finishing low to the ground, with the toe of the club closing slightly on the follow-through. The follow-through should be the same length.

Gene Mattare is the general manager and director of golf at the Saucon Valley Country Club in Bethlehem, Pennsylvania, which was established in 1920 by the Bethlehem Steel Corporation and has hosted six United States Golf Association championships. Mattare is a member of the Titleist advisory council and the Peter Millar advisory board and a five-time Merchandiser of the Year in the Philadelphia PGA of America section.

# CHAPTER ELEVEN

# Eliminating the Slice

## Brian Crowell, GlenArbor Golf Club

As far as most golfers are concerned, there is nothing quite as ugly as a slice. We all know the shot, the one that goes high and to the right (assuming we are right-handed players) and doesn't travel very far. It is often called a "banana ball." It is hideous. It is an embarrassment. It screams ineptitude, and it robs golfers of distance and dignity. It is not, simply put, very pretty.

Brian Crowell of the GlenArbor Club. Often, the only thing a slice-prone recreational golfer sees when he thinks about hitting a tee shot is a banana—a banana that reminds him of the shape of his drives.

I know about the slice all too well because I used to have one. And it was so bad that it nearly drove me from golf. Really. But I kept working on my own game and soon became the proud owner of a solid draw. I found a way to save myself from the slice and in the process discovered how I could help my students do the same.

Let's start with some basic information. A slice occurs when a golf club strikes a ball with a glancing blow that creates sidespin and causes the ball to fly weakly to the right and land with minimal roll. More than 80 percent of all golfers regularly slice the ball, making it perhaps the most widespread affliction in golf. It is also one of the most debilitating as far as scoring is concerned, for the average USGA handicap for golfers who draw the ball, moving it right to left for a rightie, is 15 strokes lower than for those who slice. Eliminating the slice can be the fastest way to lower scores and the quickest way to increase length, for a draw swing produces distances up to 30 percent greater than one that induces a slice. A golf ball hit with a draw will not only fly farther but also roll more. And there is something so much more attractive about a draw, in the way it looks and sounds, and in how it makes players feel that much better about themselves and their games. A draw connotes power and experience and a sense of being a player. A slice evokes highly contrasting sensations.

The problems of a slice are most pronounced off the tee, and poor drives put players at instant disadvantages when it comes to posting good scores and winning matches. But it can hurt you all over the course. Missing greens is part of the problem. Needing a 7-iron when your buddy is employing a wedge is also troublesome, for we all know it is easier to be accurate and precise with our approaches when we use shorter clubs. It's difficult to reach greens in regulation when you slice, and escaping rough can be a nightmare. Slicers rarely make solid contact, and that makes it so much harder to have fun on the golf course.

As bad as a slice is, and as miserable as your slice may be, there is reason to fret no longer, for I have developed a cure for the banana ball that can be achieved in three easy steps—by adjusting your setup, trusting a centered swing, and releasing in the correct fashion.

Let's start with the setup. First, figure out your target and target line. Slicers typically aim their shoulders to the left in a desperate attempt to hit the ball in that direction. But bad alignment like that only exacerbates the situation and the likelihood of making a glancing blow across the ball with your swing. Instead, you need to get your feet parallel to the target. Your knees and hips should follow suit, and that makes your base squarely aligned to where you want the ball to go. Then position your shoulders slightly closed (to the right, for righties), which will help you create draw spin, and your ball should be closer to the center of your stance. That last position comes as a surprise to most slicers, because they have a tendency to believe that having the ball closer to their forward foot will give them more time to return the clubface to square or a somewhat closed position at impact, which they think will make it easier for them to get through the ball and produce a draw—and not the dreaded slice. But if they put the ball near the middle of their stance, they actually have a much better chance of making contact with a swing coming from the inside—a swing, that is, that will produce a draw.

But don't swing yet. By aligning your shoulders more to the right and moving the ball back in your stance, you may notice that your clubface has

The first step in eliminating your slice is figuring out your target
and target line and getting properly set.

opened and is facing to the right. You must release the club, make sure the
clubface is square to your target, and then apply your grip, which will now be
in a "stronger" position. Your left thumb will have rotated to the right and be
positioned more behind the grip than on top of it, and your right hand will
follow suit. Keep in mind, though, that strong in this case refers only to the
position of the hands in the grip, not the strength with which you hold the
club. Your hands and wrists should be relaxed at all times.

And one more thing before we move onto the swing: make sure your clubface is square at address. I have found that golfers also have a habit of trying to correct their slices simply by closing the clubface, in hopes that this basic move will also induce the ball to fly right to left. But it has the opposite effect, as it forces you to come across the ball instead.

The proper setup will give you a good base from which to make a simple, centered swing with a motion that is actually smaller and very repeatable. The key in many ways is making a centered turn, not tilting forward or swaying back, and then following the shoulder line from the top of the swing and swinging to right field, as if you were standing at home plate. Do so easily, too, for if your chest and shoulders get out ahead of things and start moving to the left, you will be inclined to swing across the ball and impart that horrid slice spin. I understand that swinging to right field is hard for most veteran slicers, because they feel so sure they are going to hit the ball in that direction. But if you swing in the direction your shoulders are now positioned, if you work with the good position you have established at address, then you are set up for success, with a swing that travels out and through the ball.

With a proper setup and a centered turn, the release should come quite naturally. Energy will be delivered from the inside, and the golfer will feel balanced and strong as he turns through, to the left side. The relaxed release is critical, for slicers usually hold onto their swings with white knuckles. Do not fear the right side. Relax and let momentum finish the swing. And enjoy the pure contact that results.

Brian Crowell is the PGA head professional at the GlenArbor Golf Club in Bedford, New York, and has worked as an instructor since 1991. Over

Swing to right field if you are right-handed, and swing free.

the years, Crowell has won the Met PGA's Horton Smith Award as well as numerous honors for his teaching skills. In addition to his work at GlenArbor, he provides on-air golf commentary for major television networks and hosts and coproduces *The Clubhouse* radio show in the metropolitan New York area. Crowell has written three books, the most recent of which is *Slice-Free Golf*. More detailed information on that publication and the theories espoused in this chapter may be found at www.slicefreegolf.com.

# CHAPTER TWELVE

# Three Building Blocks

## Tim O'Neal, North Shore Country Club

I have been a member of the PGA of America since 1976 and given countless lessons over the years. During that time, I have worked hard to come up with the most effective way for my pupils to build a consistent swing. The result is a process I learned from working with top PGA instructor Chuck Cook that I use as my "three building blocks." I use

Tim O'Neal, North Shore Country Club. Photo courtesy of Kate Oelerich.

it as my basic approach to teaching, utilizing "chip," "punch," and "turn" as the so-called blocks working from impact backward.

At impact, I like to see a golfer's hands even with the front part of the front leg. That's the position in which you will find the world's best players. At the same time, I like to see the left wrist flat and the right wrist bent. The hips should be open and the shoulders, less so.

As that is the ideal position at impact, I look to teach my students to get there with their swings every time if possible. But we begin that process not with a full swing but rather the kind of swing you use with a low chip, where the hands swing about hip high to hip high, with a pitching wedge. What we are looking for here is simply *solid* contact. Start with your hands at the impact position and allow the body to pivot so that the club swings back no higher than the right hip, then turn through the ball to the other hip without using any wrists. Make sure to achieve that optimal position at impact with the hands leading and the clubhead trailing.

My goal ultimately is to grow that "chip" into a bigger swing. We take a step in that direction by using an 8-iron next, instead of a pitching wedge, and begin working on a "punch" shot, with the hands swinging somewhere between hip and shoulder high on the backswing and hip high on the follow-through. We still want the same position at impact, only now we are growing the swing. At address, the club should point at the belt buckle and continue pointing there as you start to "turn" back with the upper body. When the hands reach the right hip, as a right-handed player, the right elbow begins to bend. Once the club shaft is level to the ground it is also in line with both toes. The arms and hands gradually open the clubface as the shaft is turned up on plane due to the right elbow continuing to hinge up to about

90 degrees. The left wrist cocks and flattens as the right wrist bends back. When the hands are about chest high in the backswing, the arms and hands should be in front of the body, the left wrist flat, and the shaft pointing slightly inside the target line.

Begin the downswing by first turning the left hip out of the way and back over the left heel as the lower body separates from the lagging upper body. Starting down like this increases the coiled tension between the hips and shoulders. This critical move causes the right shoulder, arms, hands, and club to be pulled down and out toward the inside of the ball. The angle of the shaft should flatten and the clubhead lag from the inside as the right elbow moves down close to and in front of the right hip and as the wrists retain or increase their loaded and cocked condition. You should feel pressure toward the ball of your front foot. I feel that beginning the downswing in this way is the most important move during the swing.

Now, using gradually increasing speed, blend in the second half of the downswing using the following sequence. The upper body begins to uncoil as the right shoulder continues to move toward the inside of the ball. Simultaneously, the left arm will begin to break away from the upper body as the right elbow begins to unhinge and the arm to straighten. As a result, the arms and hands gradually roll the whole club out in front of you toward the inside of the ball as the clubhead begins to square up and catch up. They all continue to rotate and synchronize with your upper body "turn" through impact. At impact, the right elbow and wrist are still bent, and the left wrist is flat. The clubhead should finish low to the ground with the shaft pointing just inside the target line. The feeling is that you are hitting the ball with the "turn" of your right shoulder and upper body, using firm wrists. Even though you are using an 8-iron, your goal is to hit a low-trajectory "punch" shot with a short follow-through. Do not allow the clubhead to flip in front of your hands through impact or at the finish.

As you do this, you should be replicating the impact position and *solid* contact you were making with the "chip." Thanks to practicing the low "punch," you will hit *straighter* and more *solid* shots by being on plane with clubhead lag. What we have done here is combine the principles of *solid* and *straight* while developing two of the three essential building blocks.

At this point, it is time to move to the final building block, the "turn" back and through of the shoulders, for adding *power* and *distance*. Take a 6-iron, and begin increasing the shoulder turn in the backswing so that you can make a full swing. Keep in mind all that you have learned about being in the right place at impact (for *solid* contact) and understanding that you can work your way up club-wise all the way to a driver once you get to this stage. The ball position and stance width will change from club to club. Generally speaking, when using a driver, position the ball even with the left shoulder joint, and position the feet about your shoulders' width apart. Gradually narrow your stance and move the ball position back as the clubs get shorter in length until the ball position is about even with the left side of your face when using a pitching wedge. In addition, don't overlook the importance of having a good grip, posture, and alignment. These sound fundamentals make achieving the "three building blocks" much simpler.

After making a full upper body "turn," with the right shoulder moving back and up over the right heel, use the same downswing body rotation and sequence that you employed for the "punch." Hips go first, followed in order, with gradually increasing speed, by the right shoulder, arms, hands, and finally club. Reversing the action of the backswing, the arms, hands, and clubface now gradually close due to the straightening of the right arm and turning of your upper body. However, now with a full swing as the upper body is turning, the arms, hands, and club are fully releasing from the inside through impact with tremendous speed. Eventually, about two to four feet past impact, both arms are now straight, and the club is out in front of you. You will have a powerful feeling of releasing the entire right side of your upper body by using the right shoulder, as the arms, hands, and whole club swing through the ball with a wide follow-through after impact. The left arm forms a straight line with the shaft, which points at the left shoulder and just inside the target line. The clubface continues to close with your body "turn" as the right shoulder continues to turn up the target line. The right shoulder is now following and driving the arms, hands, and clubhead as they all synchronize and "turn" through together in plane on an arc. It should also be a priority that up to this point during the swing, the spine angle has remained fairly constant. The left elbow now begins to bend, and when the club shaft is level to the ground, it is also in line with both heels. Now, using a mirror image of the backswing, the arms and hands gradually close the clubface as the shaft is turned up on plane due to the left elbow continuing to hinge up to about 90 degrees. The shaft of the club points just inside the target line, and the right arm is straight as you gradually straighten up out of your posture. Near eye level, the right wrist cocks and flattens as the left wrist bends back. The right shoulder continues to "turn" and passes the left shoulder for a full and tall finish.

What you have done here is use the maximum amount, speed, and proper sequence of a full body rotation to help delay the release of the upper body, arms, hands, and club until they can be used most effectively at impact. Learning to arrive properly at impact, following the correct sequence, and using a full body "turn" will produce *power* in the same manner used by all the very best players. When you add the ability to swing the club on plane while controlling the clubface for improved *accuracy* learned from practicing the "punch" drill and the *solid* contact you learned from the "chip," the end result is a very strong and efficient golf swing. This is a consistent swing you can depend on that is built using the basic "three building blocks."

It is very important to note that even though we have gone into some detail in describing the "three separate building blocks," when they are blended together for the full swing, it should be a total-motion feel. This feel is very similar to a shortstop fielding a ground ball and then throwing halfway between sidearm and underhand to the second baseman when making a double play. One of my favorite drills is to take your grip on the shaft just about an inch below the grip of the club, which will run up just outside of the left hip. Practice making slow swings following the step-by-step instructions for the "chip," "punch," and "turn," making sure that the grip of the club does not touch your left hip as the right shoulder, arms, hands, and club turn through impact on the way to the finish of your swing.

To summarize, you bend the right arm and cock the wrists as the upper body "turns" while the lower body resists in the backswing. This motion loads the swing. The lower body leads and pulls the upper body, arms, hands, and club down into position during the beginning of the downswing. This motion stores the power you have just loaded during the backswing. During the second half of the downswing, the upper body "turns" toward the ball and opens to the target as the right arm straightens, allowing the arms and hands to release and square up the clubface as the wrists uncock. As the left arm swings through impact, it transfers the power created by your body, arms, and hands to the club and out into the ball. The resulting momentum now pulls the trailing right shoulder up the target line and up into the finish.

When I teach, I focus on two basic elements of the swing. Proper movement and sequence of body motion influence *solid* contact and potential *power*, while the alignments of the shaft and clubface are the major influences for *accuracy*. It is a simple way to learn and play golf. In addition, it is the most efficient way of creating the most *solid* contact, greatest *accuracy*, and desired *distance*. Remember, learn the swing first from hip to hip, then from hip to shoulder, and then above the shoulder. Approach learning in this order and you will be rewarded with a reliable and consistent swing.

Tim O'Neal is a PGA Master Professional and the head golf professional at the North Shore Country Club in Glenview, Illinois. He was Illinois Golf Professional of the Year in 2005 and won the Bill Strausbaugh Award in the Illinois PGA section two times for his mentoring of fellow PGA professionals. O'Neal has also been honored as the PGA of America's Private Club Merchandiser of the Year and qualified on two occasions and once made the final cut for the PGA National Club Professional Championship. In addition, he won the Illinois PGA Senior Masters in 2005. O'Neal has spent the past 40 years studying under the greatest instructors but credits mentor Chuck Cook as having the biggest influence on his teaching style and philosophy.

# CHAPTER THIRTEEN

# Preshot Routine and Visualization

## Mike Summa, The Stanwich Club

Mike Summa, The Stanwich Club

I have always made a point of closely watching PGA and LPGA Tour professionals whenever I have the chance to see them play in competition. I know as a teacher that there is a lot to learn from the best players in the world and a lot I can impart from those experiences to my students. I also appreciate that television tells only part of the story when it comes to the ways the professionals carry themselves in the tournaments and what they do when they compete. So much of the time on TV is focused on the actual shots they hit and very little on what they do before and after they play their shots.

I have always been interested in the preshot routine, including visualization, because the professionals do it so often and so well. One thing I've noticed is the way they look much more at the target than at the golf ball during their routines. They get behind their golf balls, they look at the target at which they are aiming, and then they visualize the shots they are going to hit. They form that vision as they look at the targets from that vantage, behind the ball, and they keep that shot visualization in their mind as they set up and stand over their shots. The best professionals see where they want to hit the ball and how they want to hit it, whether a fade or draw, whether high or low. You can see this precise preparation as you watch them in person. It's as if they are seeing their shots the way that the shot trackers lay them out on television, those video devices that track each shot and then are shown to the TV audience to demonstrate the path the golf ball takes from impact to landing. This is essentially what tour professionals are doing when they focus on their targets and not the golf balls they are about to hit. Jack Nicklaus once stated, "Before every shot, I go to the movies inside my head. Here's what I see. First I see the ball where I want it to finish in a specific small area or fairway or green. Next I see the ball going there—its path, trajectory, and behavior on landing. Finally I see myself making the kind of swing that will turn the first two images into reality. These 'home movies' are a key to my concentration and to my positive approach to every shot." I really like the focus that seems to engender, and I ask my students to take that same considered tack.

Another thing I notice as I watch top players is how they approach their golf balls after they have settled on their targets and visualized how they are going to hit the shots. They walk right down the target line from behind as they approach the ball, trying to keep their eyes over the target line as much as possible as opposed to circling around the way an amateur might. This walking down the target line best ensures seeing the line and proper alignment. So many of my students tell me they have a hard time aiming, and my response is: "We all do." Especially if we try to aim from the side instead of from behind. And poor aim leads to poor swings. So yes, getting that aim right is an important part of the preshot routine and visualization process. But it is also critical to being able to put a proper swing on the golf ball. Improper aim will clearly lead to a compensated swing in an effort to hit the ball at your target.

I like the idea of a preshot routine in large part because of the consistency it can provide to a player. We all remember the really good shots we hit, and we all want greater consistency in our games. One way we can achieve that is by making sure we do things the same way on the golf course. Preparing the same way for each shot can help instill that consistency. It can also help you get your mind right after a bad shot and during pressure situations. Watching Brandt Snedeker play his last few shots en route to winning the 2012 FedEx Cup was a good reminder how his consistent routine serves him well in pressure-packed situations. His routine through those final holes looked the same as his first tee shot of any event or, for that matter, hitting balls on the driving range as well.

To be sure, a routine does take some time, usually about ten seconds before each shot, but that's fine as long as you prepare to hit your shots while others are hitting theirs so as not to slow the pace of play. Things like selecting clubs, getting yardages, discerning winds, and selecting the targets at which you want to aim.

Each of us should develop a sound routine, and each of us should practice it, for the consistency it provides as well as the comfort, too, and the ways it can reassure us as it also assists us in maintaining and regaining focus. It creates feel and gives you as a golfer the chance to practice that feel and also to stay and be loose. It's a precursor for what you are trying to do and should become a part of your overall process.

When I think of the importance of preshot routines, I remember a time in the 1980s when I was an intern in the Dallas area. One of my coworkers was a golfer and a gambler, and he would take me to different courses on Mondays to hustle unsuspecting players. We'd have an 11 a.m. tee time, or thereabouts, and we'd get to the course nice and early so that he could walk the range and watch people hit balls, looking for players whom we would ask to join us and whom he thought we could easily beat. I did not know or understand the selection process, so I asked my friend how he singled out people. He called them "pigeons," and he said he identified them mostly by their preshot routines. He stayed away from the fellows who waggled their clubs and looked at the target before each shot with a sense of purpose and authority. But the guy who just stood there with his golf club on the ground, staring at the ball, well, that was the "pigeon" my friend wanted. That type of player didn't look like someone who knew how to stay loose and seemed instead like a person who had 17 thoughts going through his head with each swing. In my partner's mind, a player who waggled and had that preshot routine invariably had a better mental makeup and technique. And frankly, it is imperative to stay in motion by waggling and visualizing as it is much easier to start a fluid swing. *A stiff setup leads to a stiff swing*. This is clearly noticeable in other sports: The tennis professional who sways from side to side and stays light on his feet as he prepares to receive a serve from his opponent. The major-league baseball player who waggles his bat before a pitch. Staying in motion is simply more athletic and less mechanical.

And that involves every aspect of the game, from drives to fairway metal shots, from mid- and short-irons to chipping, pitching, and putting. Going to the "movies" in your mind's eye, as Nicklaus suggests, will provide the best chance of accomplishing your desired results, regardless of your level of play.

Mike Summa is a PGA Master Professional and the director of golf at The Stanwich Club in Greenwich, Connecticut. The Metropolitan PGA section named him Professional of the Year in 2012, and he has also won that organization's Bill Strausbaugh and Horton Smith Awards. *Golf Digest* has twice recognized him as the top teacher in Connecticut, and the American Junior Golf Association has honored him as its Golf Professional of the Year.

## CHAPTER FOURTEEN

# Fitness and Conditioning

## Bill Stines, Scioto Country Club

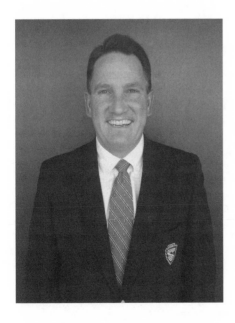

The 21st-century golf professional is an athlete. He has to be, and we see that in the golfers who are winning on tour these days. Tiger Woods started the trend in the late 1990s when he turned professional and began winning all those tournaments, and the competition quickly followed suit. They saw the difference it made

As far as Bill Stines is concerned, golfers of all ages and abilities can improve their on-course performance by being fit and well conditioned.

to be fit, as far as not only distance and power were concerned but also stamina. And if you look around the tours today, whether the PGA, LPGA, or Champions, you find the majority of those who are winning the most and who stand highest on the money lists are those who are much more in tune with their bodies than their peers were a generation ago—and much more inclined to take care of themselves. They stretch. They lift. They bike, swim, and run. They eat properly. They get plenty of sleep. They make sure they are hydrated. They are true athletes, and they are able to play and compete at the highest levels as a result.

It's the young guys on the PGA Tour, to be sure. But it is also the older fellows who have maintained their fitness, even as they have graduated to the senior circuit. As a result, they are still able to successfully knock heads with the kids. Guys like Fred Couples, who led the 2012 Masters after a couple days, even though he was 52, and ended up finishing in the top 15. Or Tom Watson, who came close in the summer of 2009 to pulling off one of the most remarkable feats in modern sports when he almost won the British Open Championship at the ripe old age of 59—and who is still able to battle the big boys on the regular PGA Tour in his 60s. Or Greg Norman nearly taking the same tournament the year before, a mere youngster then at 53. That's amazing when you think back to, say, the pre-1990 era in golf, when no one won a PGA Tour event when they were 45, Jack Nicklaus's extraordinary victory at the 1986 Masters notwithstanding. And very few over the age of 40 were even competing. Today, the fields on the regular tour are full of middle-aged guys, and they are more than holding their own, thank you very much.

The top amateur players in this day and age—the men and women who compete at elite levels in college and on the regular amateur, mid-amateur, and senior amateur circuits—are as athletic as the pros (or certainly have to be if they want to enjoy any success). And that's largely because they have seen what fitness and conditioning has meant to the touring pros—and have learned what it can do for them and their peers when they tee it up in competition.

It makes sense, then, that recreational golfers learn from those 21st-century golfers. I am not suggesting that they have to train like Navy SEALs. Nor do they have to be level-three yogis or world-class marathoners. But

It was Tiger Woods who opened everyone's eyes to the virtues of being in top physical shape, in regard to distance, power, and also stamina.

they should realize there is much they can do in this realm to improve their performance on the golf course and, ultimately, their enjoyment of the game. Just walking a few times a week and stretching for 20 minutes or so a day can make all the difference.

Fortunately, it is much easier these days for basic club golfers, weekend golfers, and social golfers to get fit and stay that way. At Scioto Country Club, where I have served as head golf professional since 2004, we have a state-of-the-art workout facility, which our members use all the time. When I hired a new assistant professional not too long ago, I made sure he was someone who had been through Titleist Performance Institute (TPI) training, which not only teaches trainees about the golf swing and club fitting but also educates them on the virtues of fitness and the ways it should be incorporated in golf. That way, he could work with our members on the range, on the course, and also in the gym. At the same time, we developed and customized workout routines for our members through the winters so that they could stay in good golf shape year-round. And in the process, we helped get these people interested not only in getting in better shape and staying that way but also in monitoring the broader ways in which they were living their lives so that they could be generally healthier and stronger.

So how do you go about getting fitter and stronger and better conditioned? It starts within the golfer and a decision he or she makes to get in better touch with his body and do things that can improve and enhance his golf life. The next step, in my view, is to go to a PGA professional for assistance. More likely than not, that person has studied a great deal about fitness and health and can help you devise a workout routine geared to your individual golf game and the things you can and cannot do physically with a golf club. TPI founders Dave Phillips and Greg Rose give seminars to

PGA professionals on the highly acclaimed teaching and fitness regimens they have developed, and that means there is an ever-growing group of club professionals who know just how to help you get fit. They can put together workout routines that will help you improve on aspects of your game that are lacking. They can assess body weaknesses arising from injury or conditions and figure out ways to build strength in those areas—and do things you have not been able to do for years.

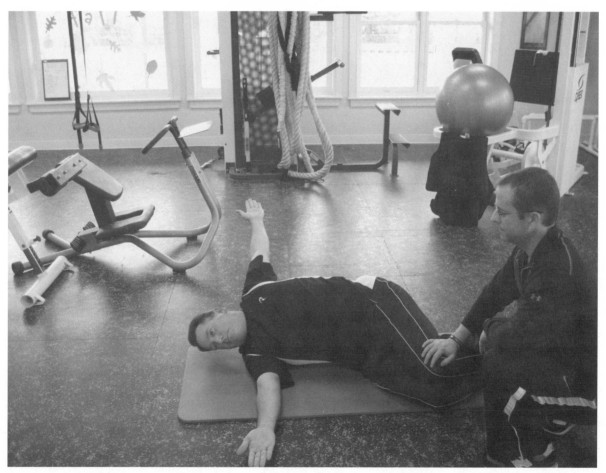

"As a golf professional, I like this trend toward fitness and conditioning because it helps my members get better and enjoy golf more."

It's that way everywhere you go. At the high school and college level, when members of golf teams work out in gyms as rigorously as they hit the practice ranges. At the golf and country clubs that have added workout facilities and instituted fitness programs.

As a PGA club professional, I like this trend toward fitness and conditioning because it helps my members get better and enjoy golf more, and it gives me another way to involve myself in their golfing lives. And the reward is not only a better relationship with them but also the chance to help someone who is 56 years old hit the ball as well as he or she did 15 years before, simply because that person is in better shape. It is a great thing to see. It's big fun to make something like that happen. And it should serve as a real example for golfers who do want to improve their performance and enjoyment of the game.

Bill Stines is the head golf professional at the Scioto Country Club in Columbus, Ohio. It is the club where Jack Nicklaus learned to play golf and has hosted five major championships, the 1926 US Open, the 1931 Ryder Cup, the 1950 PGA, the 1968 US Amateur, and the 1986 US Senior Open. In 2016, Scioto will host the US Senior Open. Prior to coming to Scioto, Stines worked as the director of golf at the Whisper Rock Golf Club in Scottsdale, Arizona, and was the head golf professional at the Pete Dye Golf Club in Bridgeport, West Virginia, and at the Honors Course in Chattanooga, Tennessee.

# CHAPTER FIFTEEN

# Course Management

## Bob Rittberger, Garden City Golf Club

I see course management simply as how a golfer works his way through a round, both mentally and physically. And the best ones do it in a way that maximizes their potential to shoot their lowest possible scores. It's an important skill and absolutely critical to success, whether you are a weekend club player, a touring

Without taking too much time, Bob Rittberger feels it is essential to analyze each shot and then make a firm decision of how and where you want to hit it. His credo is: always have a plan.

professional, or someone in between. To be sure, a guy playing on the PGA Tour is going to have such good distance control and ball location that he can overcome less-than-excellent course management, based on those tools alone. But for the rest of us, it is important to have very good plans of how to get around golf courses and to be disciplined enough to stick to those plans. It's a way for us to be mentally tough, too, and it also helps with focus.

Perhaps the first thing to consider when you think of course management is that it should be all about where *to* go, not where *not* to go. You always want to be positive here and seek how to choose the best places to put your drives, to land your approaches, to leave your chips on the green. Play to your favorite shots. Give yourself the best chance for success. If you are really good at hitting your gap wedge 100 yards and less proficient with a 54-degree wedge from 85, then leave yourself with that 100-yarder whenever possible. If you cannot reach the green of a par-4 with your second shot, don't worry. Just figure out where you can put your golf ball and give yourself the best chance at par.

Of course, it is essential to understand what your best shots are, and you do that through experience on the golf course and by keeping track of what clubs and distances bring out the best in your game. To that end, though, you can do yourself a big favor by truly knowing just how far you hit certain clubs and how far you carry them. It's not so difficult to do these days, with the distance-measuring devices that are available, and I recommend you take the time to discern how far that 6-iron really travels. And every other club in your bag.

A successful golfer knows himself and his game, and he knows both of them honestly. He knows his distances and also his tendencies. He knows whether he likes bunker shots or not. And if he doesn't, he does his best

The opening hole at the Garden City Golf Club in Garden City, New York, where Rittberger works, forces players to make an immediate decision on the length and direction of their drives, depending on what kind of an approach shot they want to hit. It brings course management into the equation right away.

to play around those hazards. He knows if he has a tendency to swing a bit faster when the wind is blowing and appreciates that when that happens, he needs to take one more club and swing more easily as he also chokes up. He comprehends that if he is having trouble with his long irons, he might want to shorten his grip on his shortest hybrid and use that instead. He also appreciates that there are certain shots he simply cannot hit and does his best to avoid them. Managing yourself and your game properly makes it that much easier to manage your way effectively and efficiently around a golf course.

I always develop a plan when I play, especially when I am competing in a tournament. I make notes, both mental and physical, of where I want to hit shots on every hole. But I also know that I must be able to adjust throughout the round and adapt not only to the way the course is playing but also to the way I am, too.

Let's discuss specifics, beginning with the way we might look at a tee shot. I typically seek out the widest, safest area to land my drives, and once I figure out where that is, I then decide whether I want to hit a driver or something shorter. Then I commit to that shot and do my best to make the best possible swing.

So many golf holes present a number of options for you off the tee, and none more so than the opening shot at the place I work, the Garden City Golf Club. The first hole is a short one, even for club players, a mere 300 yards long, and it presents a couple of possibilities on your drive. I figure it is 240 yards to reach the bunkers at the end of the fairway to the left and 220 yards to carry the waste area on the right and leave your drive in the fairway, which is the best possible position to approach the green because it is open on that side. But you have to clear an area of mounds and rather imposing rough to get there. As you consider the distance you want to hit your drive on this hole, you need to figure out what you want your second shot to be. A longer short iron? A 40-yard wedge? Do you want to run your approach onto the green from the right or pitch over the bunker on the right? Deciding on the best club off the tee is frequently a matter of deciding what is the optimal landing area for your eye and also what sort of distance and angle you want for your second shot. Knowing your game and what makes you most comfortable will enable you to make the best possible decision.

Now for the approach. Golfers often feel that it is simply good enough to hit a green in regulation, and there is merit in that thinking, as there is always a better chance for making par when you have the chance to get down in two shots with your putter. But why not try to be a bit more precise without being reckless about it? Why not give yourself the chance to make a birdie? I recommend that my members always consider the best place on the green to leave their shot. On some courses, it is critical to be below the hole. So think about that. In others, the placements of bunkers make it clear that the most unencumbered way to the putting surface is the one that does not put those hazards into play. I try to get my students to look at the type of shots they need to hit into a green as well. Is it best to fly it in the air or to run the ball up? The goal, as always, is to get on that green in regulation, and I cannot help but think of my teaching pro in college who always told me that I should try to select the approach shot to the green that requires the least amount of talent, especially in competition, for that is the shot that will invariably work best under pressure.

Of course, we are not always able to reach a green in regulation and must consider a pitch or chip to make that happen. Again, the key here is knowing your game and what you do better. Flops? Bump-and-runs? Figure that out, and make that type of shot, the one that gives you the best

Don't tempt trouble when you are on the golf course. Manage your game so that you can best avoid hazards like this bunker during your rounds.

chance to get on—and ensures at the very least a bogey. Take a moment to determine where you want to land your shot and where you want to leave it. Being closer to the green means you have a better chance of controlling the ball you are about to hit, and knowing where it should go, based on pitch, undulations, pin location, and the placement of bunkers, can make it that much easier to get up and down.

In many ways, I see course management as something that compels us as golfers to be diagnostic. Some do so from the green backward, and others from the tee forward. Figure out what is most comfortable to you, and then enjoy the time you spend doing it. Course management is another way to get into golf and really get to know and appreciate it. It is also a way to have fun with it, and even more importantly to figure out how to better succeed at it.

Bob Rittberger is the head professional at the Garden City Golf Club in Garden City, New York. A graduate of Ohio State University, he is one of the best-playing PGA professionals in the metropolitan New York area, having won the Long Island Open twice, the Long Island PGA Championship once, and the 2010 Met Open at Bethpage Black.

# CHAPTER SIXTEEN

# What We Can Learn from the Touring Pros

## Paul Marchand, Shadow Hawk Golf Club

Having spent plenty of time with touring professionals over the years, on the golf course and alongside them on the practice range, I've discovered that recreational golfers can learn a lot of things from the best players in the world—and successfully apply them to their own games. To be sure, there are certain moves that elite golfers make and different techniques they employ that are better off forgotten by everyday players,

Paul Marchand, Shadow Hawk Golf Club

because they work only for those who have the ability to compete at the highest levels of the sport. But for the most part, we can garner a lot of good information from touring pros.

One of the most interesting insights they give has to do with tendencies. All the best players in the world have tendencies. Often, they come from the way the players learned the game and the people whose swings and strokes they tried to copy. Some tendencies may have their roots in coaching techniques the players absorbed over the years or in their actual physical makeup and the things they could, and could not, do with their bodies. The same is true for 20-handicappers, juniors and seniors, teachers and weekend hackers. We all have tendencies.

I know Fred Couples very well, and he, like any other golfer, has his tendencies. One of his is for his swing to become lazy, loose, and long, which then causes him to come too much from the inside. It is something Fred has to guard against, but the good thing is he knows that is his tendency, and he works hard to keep that from happening. He know he needs to swing short and fast instead, and through the years, he has learned to recognize when he begins to get long and loose and then to correct himself.

All golfers need to be aware of the same things, of the tendencies they have and the ways they can correct the bad ones they fall into during a round. (This is also one of those cases when they need to understand that what works for a touring pro is not necessarily going to work for them and that "short and fast" is not a swing they should ever really consider.) Good players understand their tendencies and the things they must do with them, and the more the rest of us understand those same things about our own games, the better off we are. Some might have an inclination to start aiming too much to the right. Others might start swinging faster when the wind is

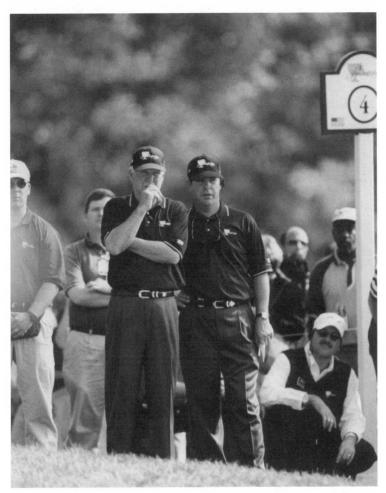

In 2000, Marchand served as a captain's assistant of Ken Venturi, who led the US President's Cup team that year. Not surprisingly, it gave Marchand a great source of learning for his teaching.

up or when they feel they need a bit more distance from a specific club. A few might make a habit of swaying over shots or moving their heads during short putts. My advice, then, is to figure out your tendencies and then figure out the best way to take care of them.

Another thing we can learn from the touring professionals is rhythm. Fred is sort of the poster child for good rhythm, even when he is swinging what we would characterize for him as "short and fast." Ernie Els and Luke Donald, too. Their cadence is so good, and the consistency of that cadence, too, and we would all be well served as golfers to have that concept of rhythm and cadence as we think about our swing while we are on the course. Good golfers have that good rhythm, that very repetitive rhythm, and it is something for recreational players to aspire to as well.

It is apparent when you watch Fred's swing, and those of other top touring pros, that they have a tremendous amount of freedom in the impact zone. They really let the club take over at that point. It is a result of their being so committed to the shot they are making, so mechanically sound with their swings, so physically able to move through the ball that way, and so free in their thinking. Stand close to a great player like Fred when he makes contact, and it sounds like a missile is getting fired at impact, although it does not seem like he is putting much effort into it at all. Average players would be wise to consider how free the tour players are at that point, because I so often see them trying to take over the impact zone themselves and control at the bottom of the swing what should actually be the free-moving part of the golf swing.

We all know about the incredible physical fitness of the men and women on tour these days, and that is something recreational golfers also should contemplate—the importance of being fit. That entails being strong, being in shape, being flexible, and I recommend that you find ways to work on all of those, if possible. It will help you play and compete better, and there are so many places to go for that kind of help. If you are already a member of a workout facility, talk to trainers there about any golf-specific exercises they can suggest. And if you are a member of a golf or country club, see

Working closely with touring professionals like Fred Couples and Colin Montgomerie (pictured here) has helped Marchand understand what it takes to succeed at that level. And many of the things Marchand has learned from champions like Monty can also help recreational golfers.

what your PGA professional might recommend. In addition, there are now plenty of golf-specific fitness centers and gyms operating throughout the country and around the world, with more opening up all the time. Of course, I understand that the average golfer does not have nearly the amount of time a professional does to work out and work on his or her physical fitness. So I am not expecting anyone who plays for fun to go that deep. But the success of the professionals in that realm and the ways they are not only able to improve their games but ensure that they can play at high levels for much longer demonstrates that it is worth finding at least some time to work on fitness and conditioning.

The short game is another obvious place where we can garner some very good knowledge from touring pros. They have long appreciated how critical that aspect of the game is, and they demonstrate that by spending roughly two thirds of their practice time hitting wedges and chips, bump-and-runs, and flops. And putts. My advice is that recreational golfers should do the same. Understand what the scoring zone is, and work on hitting the wide range of shots that must be properly made from 100 yards and closer if you have any hopes of lowering your scores.

A lot of touring pros can shoot 66 or 67 on any given day. But to do that over four rounds and four days, they have to have a very good short game. Fortunately, I have been noticing much greater awareness about how important that is. Club pros are working more with their members on their chipping and putting, and I see college coaches applying the same emphasis with their charges, making short game practice a vital part of their daily routines. Techniques are key, of course. But so is understanding your weaknesses as well as your strengths and working on them both.

Being a touring pro takes such an unbelievable amount of discipline, determination, and commitment. Their golf is their job and life, and they work on their games in ways a weekend amateur never will. Knowing what they put into their games, to say nothing of the raw talent they obviously have as well, should help you put your own game—and its shortfalls—in better perspective. You cannot possibly approach the levels of practice and dedication as the pros when you have a day job, a family, and everything else. Give yourself a break, then, when you can't pull off the miracle shot or shoot a bunch of sub-80, or even sub-70, rounds in a row. Enjoy the game and all its elements and intricacies. Have fun with your friends. Try as hard as you can to get better, understanding that as a recreational player with a busy life there is only so much time you can devote to golf. But that doesn't mean you can't keep getting better at it, by setting goals, both short-term and long-term, and working on your game when you are able to play and practice.

Finally, we need to consider club fitting. The pros have been doing it for years, on every club from their drivers to their putters, and it makes eminent good sense for you to do the same. Having clubs that are the right lie, loft, and length can make a huge difference, to say nothing of having the proper shafts. Wedges with the lofts and bounces best suited to you can take four or five strokes off an average round and make the game that much more enjoyable. Even putters need to be fit properly if you are to get the most out of them—or, should I say, *especially* putters, for putting accounts for some 40 percent of shots in a given round. Talk to your PGA professional about the best ways to get fit, and then get it done. Your game will only get better as a result.

Paul Marchand is the general manager and head golf professional at the Shadow Hawk Golf Club outside Houston. *Golf* magazine has ranked him among its top 100 teachers in America, and *Golf Digest* in its top 50. Marchand has been the longtime coach of Fred Couples, his college golf teammate at the University of Houston. He also worked for many years with Scotsman Colin Montgomerie, the Ryder Cup stalwart who won the European Tour's Order of Merit a remarkable seven years in a row, from 1993 to 1999. In addition, Marchand served as a captain's assistant to Ken Venturi during the 2000 President's Cup.

# CHAPTER SEVENTEEN

# Junior Golf

## Dave Renzulli, Country Club of Fairfield

Dave Renzulli, Country Club of Fairfield

If we truly care about golf, we care about introducing young boys and girls to the game, not only for the pleasures it brings and the life lessons it teaches but also for the long-term health of the sport itself. Problem is, juniors are not always as quick to embrace the game as we would like. So I have looked for different ways over the years to get them interested and involved with golf early on, and also to build their enthusiasm for it as they get bigger and better.

We start by recognizing there is little to gain by sending kids to practice ranges to hit balls for an hour, either in individual lessons or as parts of clinics. There simply isn't any fun in that, especially if they are new to the sport. They are whiffing on shots, topping balls, and taking huge divots. They are not seeing any positive results, and they start to get bored as a result. The fact is, you are never going to engage significant numbers of junior players with that approach.

The key, I believe, is to make things as enjoyable for them as possible. It is fine to have youngsters hit balls on the range for a bit, but we need to make it interesting, too. Mix it up. Show them how to tee up shots. Have them aim at a target, whether their golf bag or a flag, and give them shots to hit at those targets that allow them to have some success. Have them do something with each shot they make on the range. Make a contest out of getting closest to the pin.

Next, I take them to the practice putting green and make up some games they can play there. That's an aspect of golf that most kids can pick up pretty quickly and have some success with, and the little putting games you make up will keep them engaged for a while. I think it's a good idea to teach kids at that same time how to keep score, giving them something else they can do while they are trying to play—and something they can do with minimal difficulty.

I also like to take my juniors out on the golf course when I can, to show them a part of golf beyond the range and give them something new and different to see and walk. Some kids love to run in sand, so I bring them to bunkers in a fairway or by a green and let them scramble around. Then I teach them how to hit a shot out of the bunker, and then I show them how to rake the sand when they are finished. It's golf instruction, course etiquette, and recreation all wrapped into one, and they generally love doing it. I also take boys and girls onto the greens so that they can roll golf balls across the putting surfaces, first with their hands and later with their clubs, and so that they can appreciate the speed at which they roll and understand the break. Then I'll have them hit some putts, again putting together some sort of game or contest to make it fun.

I do all of that early in the process, trying to instill interest and excitement and getting the youngsters to come back for lessons and clinics. Once they get a little better, I bring them out to the course some more. The more you expose them to the course and get them off the range, the more fun they can have, and the more things about golf they can learn. Often, I have them start about 100 yards from the green. We tee up a golf ball right in the middle of the fairway and let them play in from there, keeping score so that they get into the habit of doing it. As we work on their swings and things such as stance, grip, and posture, we are also teaching them about fixing divots and pitch marks and explaining course management as they consider different approaches to the pin. We go over all sorts of short-game shots as they get around the green, bumps-and-runs, for example, short chips with their sand wedges, and maybe even a few runs at the cups from the fringe with their hybrids. We demonstrate how and when you take out the flag and tend the pin. And we do it all without any pressure and with every intention of giving them the chance to enjoy successes with golf as they also learn how to play the game.

The better they get, the more technical we can become with their swing and the more we can get into things like tempo and follow-through. The idea early on is to keep things as simple and basic as possible and to make sure their introduction to golf is as fun as possible.

I often use video when I work with kids, and that is partly because they are such visual learners and are so used to learning from and watching video. Plus, it is something else you can do during a lesson or clinic that they will likely find fun. And seeing as every junior has some sort of iPhone or Android, they can easily video their friends and their swings as they have others record theirs.

Once my junior golfers get proficient enough to play nine- and 18-hole games, I encourage them to play a tournament or two, just to get the feel for competition and the game as it is played that way and to see whether it is something they might enjoy. If I find they do like competitive golf, I take things up a notch with my teachings. Course management becomes much more of a topic, and we talk a lot about what shots to hit in certain situations. We practice up-and-downs a lot, working around greens and figuring out how to make pars when you don't hit greens in regulation. At some point, we get into the virtues of routines and how they can nurture consistency and confidence. We also talk a bit about nerves and mentally recovering from bad shots. And yes, we get more technical with the swing. At this point, I am not worried so much about boring junior golfers and losing them. If they want to play in tournaments, they are pretty much hooked. And the job from that point forward is not so much to bring them into the game but make them better.

At that point, we have ourselves a golfer.

Dave Renzulli is the head golf professional at the Country Club of Fairfield in Fairfield, Connecticut. Prior to that, he served for five years as the head golf professional at the Weston Golf Club in Weston, Massachusetts, and as an assistant professional at The Country Club in Brookline, Massachusetts.

# CHAPTER EIGHTEEN

# Specialty Shots

## Billy Anderson, Eagle Point Golf Club

We as golfers get into trouble all the time. Even if we are not the cause of such misfortunes as drivers bouncing around groves of trees or golf balls settling into a section of hardpan, we occasionally have a bit of bad luck, with tee shots rolling into old divots or balls inexplicably stopping on the sides of hills. What we have to do when those things happen is hit what I call trouble shots. They can be

Billy Anderson, Eagle Point Golf Club

challenging, to be sure, but they are something we all need to know how to do if we want to keep our scores low and win our matches or tournaments.

Before we get into how we have to hit those types of shots, let's get into why we have to do that. First of all, as golfers, we are not going to hit all of our shots down the middle of the fairway and land each approach on the green. We will invariably find trouble on the golf course through our own miscues and also through the basic vagaries of the game. It's a simple fact of golfing life, which means we need to know how to deal with it.

And while we are on the subject of dealing with trouble shots, let's also address the importance of practicing them. A golfer should never hit ball after ball on level lies on the range. He will no doubt have to hit a much wider variety of shots during an actual round, so he should practice them. Golf is a game of recall, mentally and physically, and you can help yourself tremendously by trying different types of shots on the range. Drop a few balls into divots. Try to bend an iron shot or two low and around a tree. Bang a few 7-irons off of sidehill lies and downhill lies, too. Chip some golf balls out of the woods if at all possible. Give yourself a chance to develop recall by hitting those shots in practice. Give yourself the opportunity to be comfortable on the course when you face those shots instead of having no clue.

Here's an easy question for you: Who was the greatest trouble-shot maker of all time? It has to be Seve Ballesteros, right? He made a name for himself as much for those unbelievable recovery shots that he hit time and time again as for his big tournament wins. And you have to know that he practiced those shots all the time, in all sorts of conditions and in every variation. He knew that you should never try a shot you haven't practiced. And he well understood that he would face any number of difficult lies and positions over the course of a 72-hole stroke-play tournament. He knew that he often hit shots into trouble and that if he was going to do that, he had better know how to get out of trouble, too. So he worked on that part of his game and made himself very comfortable with those types of recoveries. He didn't fear them. Rather, he saw them as opportunities to get back into a hole and to pull off shots that were as pleasurable as they were effective.

As we get into how to hit trouble shots, I think it is critical to consider them mentally and emotionally first and to take some of Seve's approaches to heart. Don't fear the recovery shots, the different and difficult plays. Rather, embrace them and the fact that you have to hit them. Focus a little harder. Commit to them. But be careful not to be reckless. Remember the great Clint Eastwood line about a man having to know his limitations. Well, that's good advice when it comes to trouble shots. Be reasonable about what you can do with a ball behind a tree or buried in a fairway bunker. Be just as happy to get back onto the fairway and ensure you make a bogey, as opposed to a double or worse, if the trouble is too great and the recovery shot so spectacular that not even Seve could pull it off. Remember, the game is all about scoring, and making bogey out of certain situations can be as good as making par.

Now let's discuss how to hit actual trouble shots, starting with those out of fairway bunkers. I suggest you always take one more club and choke down a bit on it as you dig your feet into the sand. You're getting yourself closer to the ground when you do that, and you do not want to take too much sand. Put 70 percent of your weight on your lead leg (the left leg if you are a right-handed golfer), and be sure your shoulders feel as if they are level to the ground, with your lower body quiet. Always make a downward swing to the sand, and try to hit the ball first, making sure that at the very least you get it out of the bunker.

That fairway bunker on your driving range isn't just there for show. It's a place to learn how to hit that difficult shot, one that very few golfers ever practice. Anderson thinks it's critical to consider "trouble shots" emotionally and mentally first. Don't fear them, and embrace the challenges they present.

For those trouble shots on turf when the ball is below your feet, I always choke down a bit for more control, taking one extra club if need be to compensate for the distance I will lose by doing that. I want to have a fair amount of knee flex and be able to get closer to the ball. So I feel like I am sitting down a bit more than normal. I want a little more stability, too, so I spread my feet apart a bit more. I expect the golf ball to go left to right from these lies, so I aim more to the left and try to commit to a nice, tall finish.

When the ball is above my feet, I still choke down for more control and better balance. I also do that, though, because I do not want to hit the ball fat, as there will be less distance between me and the ball than there normally is on a level lie. I know here that the shot will travel right to left as a result of the lie, so I move the ball back in my stance to compensate for that. I also aim more to the right. I try for that good balance again, with my legs a little taller than usual, and I look for a good, tall finish, too.

I think the downhill lie can be the hardest of all lies because you need to get your shoulders in line with the slope of the ground, and that is not always easy. Make sure the ball is in the middle of your stance, and try to get a sense of where your club is going to bottom out on the turf when you make your practice swings. You may want to go down a club with these lies, because they will cause it to deloft and make the ball go a bit farther than usual. Commit to a lower finish, but stay down on the ball and be sure to finish the shot properly, taking the club down the contours of the slope.

Uphill lies are perhaps the easiest of these trouble shots to hit, and your approach should be the exact opposite of that with the downhill lies. Set your shoulders and spine angle parallel with the slope, and use your practice swing to feel where the sole of your club is going to bottom out of the turf. Then, adjust your grip accordingly. You'll no doubt find yourself choking up some, again to keep from hitting the ball fat and jamming your clubhead into the ground. The ball will fly higher off these lies, so you should go up a club for greater distance. And it is a good idea to aim slightly to the right, as a right-handed player, because people most times will hit a high draw off those lies. And once again, commit to the finish.

Two of the toughest lies to deal with are those on bare ground, or hardpan, and also in divots. On hardpan, put the ball into the middle of your

Anderson believes that uphill lies are the easiest of the trouble shots, and one of the keys to success with these is using your practice swing to feel where the sole of the club is going to bottom out of the turf.

stance, with most of your weight, as a righty, on your left side at address. Be sure your grip pressure is even, and hit down and through the ball, hitting the ball first and then the ground.

When a ball rolls into a divot, you should make much the same swing, maybe taking an extra club and making a steeper strike on the ball with a shorter follow-through, letting the club do the work.

Billy Anderson has been the director of golf at the Eagle Point Golf Club in Wilmington, North Carolina, since 1999. During that time, he has won the North Carolina and South Carolina Opens as well as the North Carolina PGA Championship. In 2011, the American Junior Golf Association (AJGA) named Anderson its Golf Professional of the Year.

# CHAPTER NINETEEN

# The 19th Hole

## Gene Mattare and John Steinbreder

Gene Mattare

Up to now, this book has devoted time and space to giving golfers 18 ways to play a better 18 holes. But there is more to the royal and ancient game than mere birdies and bogeys and grinding one's way around a course. Golf is also about having fun, whether you are playing by yourself, competing in a weekend four ball with your friends, or teeing it up in a tournament. And while the links may be where fun is most often found, we believe an equally enjoyable spot is the bar or pub where golfers gather after their rounds, the terrace or grill room where drinks are shared and stories told. Those spots are much better known as "19th holes," and we fervently believe the warmth and conviviality they offer are such a positive part of the overall golf experience—and so soothing to the golfing soul—that they can only help a person improve as a player as well. That's why we are compelled to include a chapter on them in this volume.

Though no one seems to be exactly clear when the term "19th hole" was first used, an early 20th-century book titled *The Nineteenth Hole: Being Tales of the Fair Green* popularized it. And slowly but surely the expression worked its way into the golfing vernacular. One writer around the time of World War I discussed the "Kingdom of the 19th Hole" and described a fellow residing in that realm as a "Philosopher Extraordinaire and Authority Unquestioned." The virtues of the 19th hole were recognized even more clearly in a 1920 publication by George Ade called *Hand-Made Fables* that stated: "Golf will make you forget everything but the 19th hole." Some years later, a writer for the *Daily Express* averred: "Most courses have been completely unplayable, except at the nineteenth hole." And we agree with the bloke who wrote in the mid-1970s: "Around every nineteenth hole, legends are recalled of astonishing shots."

We have long felt that the 19th hole is a critical part of a proper golf experience. It is a wonderful place to kick back after a good walk, whether it was spoiled or not by poor play, and recount the round with your golfing mates. And lingering in such a pleasant retreat puts a veritable bow on top of the awesome gift that is a round of golf.

Not surprisingly, we have our views as to what makes a 19th hole great, and there are several factors that come into play. Start with location. A 19th hole rises high in our eyes when it overlooks a finishing hole, as is the case with the one at, say, the legendary Garden City Golf Club on Long Island, where chairs and tables are arrayed on a sweeping flagstone terrace by the green of the par-3 18th. Or at the Country Club of Fairfield in Connecticut, where a porch is perfectly perched behind the final green at that links-style course. From that vantage, golfers can gaze down that testy par-4 finisher, look across other portions of the celebrated Seth Raynor track, and savor the views of Long Island Sound beyond. Then there is the 19th hole on the awning-covered patio in back of number 18 of the Old Course at Gene's retreat, the Saucon Valley Country Club in eastern Pennsylvania. We like how those locales allow players to watch other groups come in while they enjoy their drinks in very scenic settings—and occasionally heckle fellow duffers standing over crucial chips and putts. And we appreciate the ways 19th holes create environments that engender comfortable conversation among friends and put just the right touches of what have been wonderful days on the links. They also serve to ease the transition from the course itself to the real world that exists beyond the borders of the layout that has just been played.

While those outside settings can be very enticing, we are also big fans of 19th holes that are inside. There is something so appealing about those housed in classic locker rooms, like the high-ceilinged sanctuary at the Seminole Golf Club in Juno Beach, Florida. And we could sit for hours on the overstuffed couches and chairs there, talking golf, sipping drinks, and looking up occasionally at the boards on the walls listing tournament winners over the years. Many of the most prominent names in the professional and amateur game are there—Ben Hogan and Arnold Palmer, Billy Joe Patton and Vinny Giles—and they evoke a pleasing sense of history. So do spots like The Country Club in Brookline, Massachusetts, which has memorabilia from the many majors it has hosted over the years hanging on the weathered, wood-paneled walls of its cavernous men's locker room. Just as appealing is the way the intimacy and privacy of the round itself is preserved in those places, and the robustness of four men sharing a game together lasts a little longer as a result.

John Steinbreder

Some of our favorite 19th holes feature museum-like settings or boast the feel of a classic pub or bar. Again, Garden City quickly comes to mind, and when you step off the terrace there and into the clubhouse, you find den-like clusters of rooms displaying old photographs, burnished trophies, vintage books, and classic golf clubs. Another keeper is the superlative Prestwick Golf Club in Western Scotland, where a sitting room with great picture windows looking onto the course that hosted the first 12 British Open Championships feels like an Edwardian library with a special focus on golf. A man without much of a schedule can happily tarry there for hours after a game, reading through volumes of Bernard Darwin, for example, or scouring old scorecards from matches long gone by.

Yes, location is important. And the 19th holes that are best situated also have a way of boasting other elements that are as key to the ultimate postround retreat. A sense of golf history, to be sure. Ambience, too, and the feeling of total comfort that envelopes a great watering hole and embraces its patrons with warmth and cheer. Good service is always appreciated, and the guys who draw perfect ales and pour potent drinks—and also keep you grinning with well-timed repartee—make a postround beverage taste that much better. And to be fair, it doesn't really matter whether a place is part of an actual golf club or not, like the bar at Dunvegan Hotel in St. Andrews, Scotland, a small, *Cheers*-like institution situated just off the 18th green of the Old Course. Deftly run and presided over by Texas Aggie Jack Willoughby and his lovely Scottish wife, Sheena, it exudes an ethos as intoxicating as that of the links itself. And golfers have been known to spend as much time in St. Andrews at that beguiling spot as they do on the courses themselves.

Then there are the drinks. All great 19th holes have an equally great signature drink, whether it's a Dark and Stormy in the wood-paneled bar at the Mid Ocean Club in Bermuda or a Transfusion on the patio at the Oakmont Country Club outside Pittsburgh. Nothing tastes quite as good as a Southside on the deck of the Stanford White–designed clubhouse at Shinnecock Hills or in the screened-in porch retreat called the Birdcage at the historic National Golf Links of America just down the road. Ditto a gin and ginger ale at the Sunningdale Golf Club outside London. The rum punch lovingly called a Fernando (after the man who makes them so well) at The Country Club is the sort of mixological triumph about which arias are composed, and we feel the same way about the Whisky Macs at Prestwick, delectable concoctions made of equal parts whisky and something strange and fantastic called Crabbie's Green Ginger Wine.

As a rule, we believe that it is always better to eat and drink what is local, which is why we go to signature drinks when that choice is there. And even if a place does not have a club or course drink per se, we still try to take our cues from the overall environs. Guinness on tap in any Irish 19th hole works pretty well for us. So does single malt whisky at a Scottish club or course.

There is no way we can guarantee that proper use of the 19th hole will take strokes off your game, make you swing as well as Rory McIlroy, or fill the family coffers with winnings from Sunday morning closeouts. But we do believe a good one creates very special experiences, even if the only thing you are drinking up postround is the atmosphere. And they go a long way to making the great game of golf even better.

# Acknowledgments

I have been around golf most of my life, which means I have spent a lot of time with the PGA professionals who teach, promote, and explain the sport at clubs and courses around the world. And I fervently believe they are among golf's greatest assets. As a rule, they are athletes who love to play the royal and ancient game. They also enjoy bringing others into golf, and their skills as educators in all aspects of the sport are something to behold. I admire their patience and resilience and the selfless way these professionals give of themselves to golfers of all ages and abilities, whether it is stopping by the range to offer a tip between shots; finding them just the right shirt, glove, or golf shoes in their shops; or explaining the intricacies of club fitting and why one type of iron may make more sense than another for a particular player. They organize club tournaments with all the enthusiasm and efficiency of a US Open. They massage fragile egos and nurture nascent players. In the private club world, they deal with political circumstances so difficult and inane they can drive even the sanest soul mad. And they somehow manage to do it all with grace and calm and smiles on their faces. They are called professionals for a reason.

PGA professionals are in many ways the backbone of golf, and they are certainly the ones who make this book, *18 Ways to Play a Better 18 Holes*, as compelling a volume as it is. That is why I am dedicating a good portion of these acknowledgments to the 18 professionals who contributed to this book, so that I may properly thank them for their help and also for their keen insights into so many aspects of the game. Most of them are good personal friends as well as professional contacts, and they have made my job as a golf writer over the years, and my frequent role as America's guest when it comes to playing their golf courses, pure delight. I will be forever grateful for their assistance as well as their friendships and the many ways they have enhanced my life. I am also sure that readers of this book will feel just as warmly toward them after reading all the salient and easy-to-comprehend things they have to say.

Rick Rinehart of Rowman & Littlefield is not much of a golf instructor, but he is one hell of a book publisher, and I must also express my profuse thanks to him for believing in this idea and giving me every opportunity to execute it. This is not the first time we have worked together, and it certainly will not be the last. In fact, I am already looking forward to our next project.

Then, of course, there is my family, and there is no way this book makes it to print without their unending love and understanding. My wife,

# ACKNOWLEDGMENTS

Cynthia, cheerfully supports me through the long days and nights I toil at my desk, as she also runs our household and her own business to boot. And our daughters, Exa and Lydia, charm us with their warmth and wit and keep us smiling as they also keep us on our toes. I could not be more pleased to be with them and to have them all around nor more grateful for the many ways they take care of me, especially in the midst of a few book projects.

John Steinbreder
*Redding, Connecticut*

# Index

# About the Author

**John Steinbreder** is an award-winning journalist and the author of 16 books. He works as a senior writer for *Global Golf Post* and contributes to Masters .com, the official website of the Masters Tournament. Previously, Steinbreder was employed as a reporter for *Fortune* magazine, a writer/reporter for *Sports Illustrated*, and a senior writer for *Golfweek*. He has also contributed to several prominent periodicals over the years, including the *New York Times Magazine*, *Departures*, *Forbes Life*, and *Golf Digest*. An avid golfer who carries a USGA index of six, Steinbreder has reported on the game on five continents and received 10 honors for his work from the Golf Writers Association of America, and 12 from the International Network of Golf. He lives in Redding, Connecticut, with his wife, Cynthia, and their daughters, Exa and Lydia.